WHEN GOD WRITES YOUR LIFE STORY

Eric & Leslie Ludy

Multnomah Books

WHEN GOD WRITES YOUR LIFE STORY
published by Multnomah Books
A division of Random House, Inc.

Published in association with Loyal Arts Literary Agency, LoyalArts.com
© 2004 by Winston and Brooks, Inc.
International Standard Book Number: 978-1-59052-339-1

Cover image by Harald Sund/Getty Images

Unless otherwise indicated, Scripture quotations are from:
New American Standard Bible © 1960, 1977, 1995
by the Lockman Foundation. Used by permission.

Other Scripture quotations are from:
The Holy Bible, New King James Version (NKJV)
© 1984 by Thomas Nelson, Inc.
The Holy Bible, King James Version (KJV)

Multnomah is a trademark of Multnomah Books,
and is registered in the U.S. Patent and Trademark Office.
The colophon is a trademark of Multnomah Books.

Printed in the United States of America

For information:
MULTNOMAH BOOKS
12265 ORACLE BOULEVARD, SUITE 200
COLORADO SPRINGS, CO 80921

Library of Congress Cataloging-in-Publication Data

Ludy, Eric.
  When God writes your life story / Eric and Leslie Ludy.
      p. cm.
  Includes bibliographical references (p. 236).
  ISBN 1-59052-339-3
  1. Christian life—Meditations. I. Ludy, Leslie. II. Title.
  BV4501.3.L862 2004
  248.4—dc22

                                    2004009994

          09 10—10 9 8 7 6 5 4

Contents

part one
DREAMING THE IMPOSSIBLE
Passionately Pursuing a God-Scripted Life

part two
LIVING THE IMPOSSIBLE
Practically Achieving a God-Scripted Life

part three
FRONTIER FIELD GUIDE
A Study Guide for Shaping the Inner Life

When a soul sets out to find God it does not know whither it will come and by what path it will be led; but those who catch the vision are ready to follow the Lamb wherever He goes, and it is as they follow, obedient to what they have seen, in this spirit of joyful adventure, that their path becomes clear before them, and they are given the power to fulfill their high calling. They are those who have the courage to break through conventionalities, who care not at all what the world thinks of them, because they are entirely taken up with the tremendous realities of the soul and God.[1]

BISHOP BARDSLEY

Eric

A h, the joys of living in Colorado! I just finished shoveling a foot of snow off our driveway which, in a strange way, I sort of enjoyed. Shoveling snow makes me feel like a rugged mountain man. (Of course, the fantasy dies the moment I look in a mirror.)

In Colorado, risk and excitement are always right outside your front door. It's really the perfect place to write a book about experiencing the ultimate adventure. To be honest, though, Leslie and I hardly qualify as adventurers—at least, not in the Rocky Mountains sense of the word. We aren't really kayaking, ice-climbing, sleep-on-the-edge-of-a-cliff kind of people. We have lots of friends who are wild-eyed thrill seekers, but their bungee-jumping lunacy hasn't rubbed off on us.

It's not that we haven't tried. We've spent plenty of time sleeping on the hard ground, waking up to subzero temperatures, brushing our teeth with canteen water, trying to develop a love of camping. But personally, we just can't figure out why people think this stuff is fun.

On one such "adventure," Leslie and I awoke to the sounds of growling and grunting just outside our tent, where a huge bear was searching for the chocolate-covered peanuts we forgot to hide up in a tree before going to bed. I still hold that my noticeable quaking that morning was from the cold mountain air, not the fear of a wild beast attack. Leslie doesn't believe me.

Then there was the time I let my brother-in-law talk me into a multiday mountain trek. I came home feeling like an arthritic old man. My condition probably had something to do with the three sleepless nights I had spent lying on the hardest, rockiest, most unforgiving ground this side of Granite Mountain.

Sure, it's great to spend time with friends and family, enjoying the beauty of nature. But we would much prefer to do it from a cozy ski lodge with a roaring fire and a big picture window.

Leslie and I choose to be "crazy" in different ways. We really *do* have a craving for adventure and for living on the edge—just not the kind of adventure that involves fleeing from an avalanche on skis or dangling from the side of a mountain on a frayed rope. Instead, we take our risks in the realm of living life. Our adventures aren't isolated to our hobby time or vacation getaways; they are woven into the fabric of our everyday existence.

The Adventure of a Lifetime

Colorado is bursting with people who are actually *eager* to leave the comforts of home and sleep on a rock for the night, using the cold mountain river as their bathtub in the morning. And a number of them are more than willing to live that way for an entire week. Some even have the fortitude to do it for a whole month.

But are there any today willing to live that way for a *lifetime?*

Therein lies the challenge of this book. This is a message that calls us to enter the most dramatic adventure of all time—an adventure that far surpasses the reckless expeditions of the most ambitious mountain explorer. It's an adventure that will claim our entire existence. This adventure means saying *adios* to life as we know it. Yet it also means discovering life the way it was meant to be lived, in all its breathtaking wonder and grandeur.

The message of this book is deeply meaningful for both of us. It has been shaped through the personal fires of testing, the valleys of failure, and the mountaintops of triumph. It is a message that has molded us into *true* adventurers. *God's* adventurers. This message has forever changed our lives, and we believe it can forever change yours as well.

Leslie and I have talked with countless young people who are asking the *Who? What? When? Where? Why?* and *How?* questions about life. *Who* am I? *What* am I here for? *Where* am I supposed to be headed with my life? *When* am I going to do my first really big thing that makes the whole world stand up and take notice? *Why* is my life so mediocre, even though I'm trying to make it grand? *How* can I live a life that really counts?

These are life questions. We all have them. God etched these questions upon the tablet of our beings. He gives us these question marks that cause us to search for answers. He prompts us to ask so that He can answer.

God wants us to know who we are. He wants us to know why we are here on this earth, and He wants to give us a clear direction for our life. He wants to do big things in and through us. He wants to direct us out of the swamps of mediocrity and into the mountains of heroism, training us to live a life that truly counts.

Our goal is to give you the foundation stones of a truly heroic Christian life. This book is not for those who put a high value on comfort and ease. It's written for those who are ready to do whatever it takes for their life to truly mean something. We don't pretend to wax eloquent on points of philosophy here. We merely seek to stay true to Scripture and present the practical steps necessary for exploring the vast wild lands of God's enormous expectations for our lives.

Some Things to Consider

As we begin our journey, here are a few details to keep in mind.

In the first half of the book, we attempt to lay out a vision for what a successful Christian life really looks like—what it really means to live life to the fullest. The second half of the book is more of a field manual, a practical study guide for your personal use or for use in a group setting. This section is outfitted with practical steps to help you further realize this message in your own life.

In these pages, we use many illustrations and quotes from people we have encountered throughout our life and ministry. When necessary, names have been changed and some descriptions and stories have been adapted to protect the privacy of those involved.

The subject of a God-scripted life is gigantic in scope and is impossible to fully explore in a single book. Please feel free to visit our website, www.whenGodwrites.com, where you can access additional material that can help you take these truths even deeper.

And now, we invite you to strap on your hiking boots, fill up your super-sized water bottle, and allow us to introduce you to the Author of adventure. This is a book of action. It's about packing up your tent, rolling up your sleeping bag, shaking off the sludge of mediocrity, and heading into unknown territory on a life-changing expedition. It is our hope that this book will fan into flame your desire to live this life to the fullest and provide you with the practical tools to do so.

With great love and expectancy, we dedicate this book to those in our generation who are seeking a spark from the roaring campfire of God. If you are ready to experience the most amazing, invigorating, inspiring, and satisfying drama of all time, get ready to discover how breathtaking the adventure can be when God writes your life story.

part one

DREAMING THE IMPOSSIBLE

Passionately Pursuing a God-Scripted Life

Ah, but a man's reach should exceed his grasp,
or what's a heaven for?[2]
ROBERT BROWNING

God's dreamers are always unpractical,
but in the end…their dreams come true.[3]
AMY CARMICHAEL

one

Eric

THE ENDLESS FRONTIER

awakening the inner pioneer

> *We have a God who delights in impossibilities*
> *and who asks, "Is anything too hard for Me?"*[4]
>
> ANDREW MURRAY

What happened to our little-kid passion for achieving the impossible? When did we stop shooting for impossible goals and start aiming for realistic targets instead? As little kids, we dream of a bigger-than-life existence. But eventually we grow up. We lose our "oomph" to keep aiming high. We settle for everyday mediocrity. We stop trying to be heroic and finally accept being average.

Eric Ludy: The Bionic Man

When I was seven years old, I *was* the Six Million Dollar Man. No joke! I was none other than Steve Austin: Bionic Man. Heartthrob and human machine.

For those of you who didn't have the privilege of growing up in the bionic era of the 1970s, Col. Steve Austin was the ultimate rendition of coolness and technology rolled into one. Equipped with a pair of nuclear-powered legs, one bionic arm, and a bionic eye, Steve Austin could perform incredible feats of strength and speed—usually filmed in slow motion with distinctive high-tech sound effects—while battling foreign spies, nefarious megalomaniacs, extraterrestrial villains, and in my favorite episode, a bionic Bigfoot!

And I, little Eric Ludy, had the amazing talent of transforming my puny seven-year-old body into a superhuman bionic machine whenever I felt the urge. I *was* the original Bionic Man.

Then my buddy Donny had the gall to declare that *he* was Steve Austin, too.

"I'm Steve Austin!" Donny would shout, pointing to his *Six Million Dollar Man* T-shirt as definitive proof.

"No, *I'm* Steve Austin!" I argued as I ran in slow motion to Donny's mom's garden and lifted a ten-pound rock while imitating the famous bionic man machine noises.

The obvious truth that we couldn't bring ourselves to accept was that neither of us was *anything* like Steve Austin. The Six Million Dollar Man could leap over fifteen-foot electrified fences in a single bound, toss a boulder like it was a football, and read the bottom line on the eye chart from three miles away. Donny and I could barely jump high enough to reach the lowest branch on his parents' weeping willow. We could scarcely muster up enough strength to carry a laundry basket full of clothes down the hall, and both of us were flunking eye tests by the first grade.

Nevertheless, I wholeheartedly believed that I was the one and *only* Steve Austin on Maple Lane. Donny was merely an imposter. And yet he remained convinced that *he* was the real deal and that I was the imposter.

"You're *not* the Bionic Man!" I yelled. "You can't jump more than three feet!"

"Well, you can't even lift Drool off the ground!" Donny shouted back, referring to his one-eyed mutt that really *did* drool.

Donny's mom chose that moment to interject a sobering piece of information into the pandemonium: "Boys, I hate to break it to you, but *neither* of you is the Bionic Man!"

Eventually, I traded my bionic sound effects for Superman Underoos that transformed me into the red-caped wonder. I went through a phase where I became the Hulk, decapitating my sister's Raggedy Ann doll in one of my displays of phenomenal strength. And finally, to top off my youthful career as a superhero, I became Luke Skywalker, rescuing Princess Leia with my powerful lightsaber (actually a toilet plunger).

Dreaming the Impossible

Yes, this was all just little-kid make-believe. Most of us reminisce on our days of childish wonder and innocence with a sigh and a chuckle. But we also look back upon our wee selves and shake our heads, wondering what ever possessed us to pursue such heroism, such grandeur, such amazing displays of superhuman activity? What caused us to try to become something so far beyond who we really were?

As little kids, we gravitate towards the impossible like moths to a flame. While the older and "wiser" among us are caged in by their knowledge and maturity, little kids are free to dream impossible dreams and pursue impossible lives.

In our little-kid passion, we want to wear the tennis shoes with the blue swoosh stitched into the side so we can jump over tall buildings. We insist on eating the cereal that will enable us to run faster than a speeding locomotive. And we know which brand of bread will enable us to lift cars off the ground like Superman or repel bullets like Wonder Woman.

So what happened to our little-kid passion for achieving the impossible? When did we stop shooting for impossible goals and start aiming for realistic targets instead? As little kids, we dream of a bigger-than-life existence. But eventually we grow up. We lose our "oomph" to keep aiming high. We settle for everyday mediocrity. We stop trying to be heroic and finally accept being average.

As we grow up, the world tells us that aiming our lives at the impossible only leads to disappointment. Somewhere along the way, we are persuaded to loosen our grip on our dreams and pitch our tents in the land where everyday humans dwell.

Disabled Dreams

Our generation is all too familiar with disabled dreams. The things we long for most in life are the very things we believe cannot be achieved.

Max, a college sophomore from Michigan, has given up on finding fulfillment in life. "I used to think that someday I would wake up with a sense of purpose," Max told me recently, "but now I have just accepted that my life will always feel confusing and pointless."

Krista, a twenty-five-year-old skier, has given up her search for a beautiful love story. "When I was little, I dreamed about falling in love with someone who was my best friend, and having an incredible marriage that lasted a lifetime," she recalled wistfully. "But after seeing so many marriages fall apart, I really think that lasting love is just a myth."

Wyatt, an eighteen-year-old computer gamer, has given up believing that real-life family relationships can be healthy and strong. "I watch reruns of *The Cosby Show* and think how unrealistic that is," he said. "I mean, every family in the world is a dysfunctional mess. Why pretend things can ever be different?"

When our little-kid passion for the impossible dies, everything worth living for slowly suffocates as well. We give up our hopes of finding a sense of victorious fulfillment and purpose in each day; of making a dynamic difference in this world; of discovering a love that lasts a lifetime; or of enjoying enduring friendships. And most of us give up hope of ever being on intimate terms with God. We scoff at the idea of experiencing a passionate love affair with the King of the Universe that transforms our existence.

Of course, some might argue that giving up on these dreams might be for the best. After all, if you never aim high, you'll never be disappointed with mediocrity. When you aim for the impossible, you are usually misunderstood, ridiculed, and alienated. So why live a life of risk and challenge when a life of security and ease is sitting on your front doorstep? Why choose a way of life that all the sane people on earth have already rejected?

But what if our so-called impossible dreams are not impossible at all?

Cheap Hollywood Imitations

When you look around at Christians today, it's hard to believe that throughout human history Christ-followers have always been the biggest dreamers of impossible dreams. But it's true! Ancient Christians were known for pursuing the inconceivable. Nowadays, Christians seem far more interested in living comfortably, being well respected, and guarding their 401(k) plans than in tackling the impossible. But once upon a time, it was actually Christ-followers who found supernormal pleasure in defying the odds.

From early Rome to communist China, Christ's children have cherished every looks-like-there-is-no-hope circumstance, because it was on those very occasions that God burst forth with awe-inspiring power. If ever it seemed all hope was lost, it meant the almighty God of the Universe was near.

After all, Tom Cruise didn't invent the dazzling smile in defiance of hopeless circumstances. God did. Arnold Schwarzenegger was not the first to exude confidence in a life-and-death conflict. That was God. Russell Crowe's indomitable spirit in the face of extreme danger? Mel Gibson's fearlessness in battle? Yep. God's too! Our God invented the superconquering life. He raised up the original bigger-than-life action heroes.

Throughout the centuries, God has been in the business of building astonishing lives, lives that "by faith conquered kingdoms, performed acts of righteousness, obtained promises, shut the mouths of lions, quenched the power of fire, escaped the edge of the sword, from weakness were made strong, became mighty in war, put foreign armies to flight."[5]

But somehow, we Christians lost our once-great passion

for the impossible. And in so doing we stopped expecting our God to be the God of the impossible.

Nowadays, most of us gravitate *away* from difficulty. Sitting in a movie theater, we are thrilled when Arnold or Tom ends up in an impossible situation because we trust the movie's director to somehow turn it into a happy ending. But we melt with fear when we find *ourselves* in an impossible situation in life, because we don't trust God as our life's Director to come through for us and create a triumphant ending. We don't know our God as the God of the Impossible.

But what is a movie without a conflict? Where's the drama without a mountain of impossibility to climb? The very thing that makes for an exciting story is the same thing that makes for a wonderful and amazing life: *overcoming the impossible*. For life to be fully lived, it must wrestle the impossible and win. For life to be fully lived, the God of the Impossible must be fully trusted with the writing of the script.

God wants to blow our minds with His crazy plot turns and last-minute heroics. Instead, we have settled for ordinary lives written by ordinary human hands—life as a cheap and boring counterfeit of what could be. Our Christian lives sadly play like PBS documentaries on the history of saddle stitching rather than awe-inspiring epic adventures. It seems Hollywood is the only place we find conquering, heroic lives these days.

Real-Life Action Heroes

Even though we know that Hollywood is make-believe, deep down we still want to live real life as large as the movies. As little kids we didn't aspire to be a business executive with two weeks' paid vacation a year, a corner office with a view, and a healthy pension at the age of sixty-five. We wanted to be CIA operatives, Jedi masters, samurai warriors, or at least a Mr. Smith who goes to Washington. And deep down, we still do! We want to be someone who makes a difference—someone who puts a dent in life before we leave it.

Maybe it's my melodramatic tendencies, but I believe that God wants our lives to display a little more cinematic magic and a little less mediocrity. I don't mean the hip attitude and the morally debased climate of Hollywood, but the larger-than-life hero mentality of the silver screen. And I don't mean lives without problems, but rather, lives *overcoming* problems.

Modern Christians have focused so much on God's loving us in our weakness that we seem to have forgotten that He wants to build each of us into walking, talking, world-changing demonstrations of His amazing grace. God designed us to become true modern-day heroes—men and women who are devoted, courageous, fearless, immovable, and marked with uncompromised integrity.

God is in the business of making heroes: heroes that Hollywood is incapable of imagining. He is in the business of writing amazing scripts for our lives. Not Hollywood scripts, but *heavenly scripts* that shape us into His real-life action heroes.

Stepping into an Endless Frontier

For some reason, my little-kid quest for the impossible carried over into my young adult years. Throughout high school, though I no longer fancied myself the Bionic Man or the Incredible Hulk, I was absolutely convinced that I possessed a mesmerizing singing voice that rivaled Frank Sinatra's. It wasn't until college that I found out the truth about my vocal talent—or lack thereof.

As I was warbling out one of my patented sappy love songs to an unwitting young lady, my track coach broke the news to me.

"Ludy, you're terrible!" he informed me rudely.

"What do you mean, I'm terrible?" I asked, hoping he was referring to my ability to tie my shoes and not, God forbid, my *singing voice*.

"When you sing, you sound like Elmer Fudd being given a wedgie!" he stated coldly, not a hint of humor in his voice.

At that moment, my dream of becoming the next lead singer for REO Speedwagon came crashing to the ground. But God had a plan for my voice, even when the rest of the world was shouting, "Shut that guy up!" And it was my musical journey that awakened me to the secret of a God-scripted life.

God took the pen of my life and wrote a chapter entitled, "Someone Please Hurry Up and Teach This Guy How to Sing." And Scott, an ambitious vocal trainer, was the unfortunate soul who took on the job. Scott is not your everyday, run-of-the-mill vocal coach. He is one of the world's very *best*. It's ironic that I, a musical disaster waiting to happen, would end up being trained by a master like Scott. But for some reason, in a kindhearted display of compassion, Scott took me under his wing.

"Eric, if you want to be great at something, you must devote yourself to it," he told me sternly. "If I am going to work with you, you need to commit to six hours a day of vocal training."

Six hours?! Was he crazy? Who in this world has six

hours each day to give to singing? Scott's simple reply was, "Those who are the very best."

Scott used to train Olympians how to increase their oxygen intake up to three times with every breath. He took the athletic approach towards vocal training.

"How many miles did you run this week?" Scott would ask at our weekly training sessions. At my reply he would bellow, "Come on, you wimp! You've only just begun to get in shape! Show me your abdominal strength."

I would get down on the floor, and he would count out a ridiculous number of leg lifts and sit-ups. "Come on, you pansy! I work with old ladies who have more ab strength than you!"

In spite of his foot-to-the-rear style of teaching, Scott was truly one of the most lovable men I've ever met. He never let me leave his office without a hug. But as kind as he was, he never gave me a compliment. He never gave me any indication that I had finally risen out of the ashes of Elmer Fuddism.

After a year of Olympian training, I grew restless with a gnawing need for Scott to tell me how good a singer I had become. Was I a true singer yet? Or did my voice still sound like the horrid screech that precedes a train wreck?

"Scott," I sheepishly muttered one day, trying to hide my embarrassment at the question I was about to pose. Awkwardly, I shoved out the words that I had been practicing within my mind over the past three months. "How *good* am I?"

"What do you mean?" Scott studied me calmly, enjoying my discomfort.

"Uh," I squirmed. "Um, how good of a singer am I?"

Scott was thoughtfully silent for a few long moments, a cryptic Gandalf-like expression written across his face.

"Eric," he finally said, "you played soccer growing up, didn't you?"

"Yeah," I answered, not quite catching what this had to do with my singing talents.

"When did you start playing soccer?"

"I don't know. I guess I was probably seven."

"Think back to when you were seven years old and you had been playing soccer for one month. How good were you?"

"I stunk!" I answered without hesitation.

"Exactly!" Scott rang happily.

I stood there in stunned silence. Despair whirled inside my head. *After a year of intense training, I still stunk? All my hard work had been for nothing?*

But before my self-deflating was complete, Scott interjected a powerful piece of wisdom. "Eric," he said earnestly, "There is something you need to understand. Singing is an *endless frontier*. It is a frontier that *no one* has reached the end of or fully explored. You have taken *one step* into this endless frontier, and you are asking me how far you have gone." With that, he threw his hands up in the air and chuckled, "Well, you've only taken one measly step!"

I chewed on his words with new interest. I had never heard anyone describe the art of singing that way, as a limitless horizon. I had always assumed that with a little hard work, I could achieve the status of a true singer and my journey would be over.

But according to Scott, nothing could be further from the truth.

"I want you to realize something," Scott continued sincerely. "You have taken one step into the endless frontier of singing. And you are now one step further into this frontier than 99.9 percent of the human race. But don't be satisfied with just one step. Don't settle for just being above average. *Never* pitch your tent. Until you have explored the outer reaches of this endless frontier, *never* stop your pursuit of excellence!"

What If There Is More to the Christian Life?

I learned more from Scott that day than simply the proper attitude of an excellent singer. I gained a vision for the essence of true living.

As modern Christians, we are used to pitching our tents. We learn the basics and assume that's all there is to know. Tragically, most of us never realize that the art of living is meant to be a boundless adventure beyond our wildest dreams.

We read a few Bible verses, sing a few worship songs, and convince ourselves we have reached the spiritual maturity of Paul the apostle. We get one step ahead of the culture and then, for some strange reason, *stop all forward movement*. The majority of us may be one step ahead of the world when it comes to purity, spiritual disciplines, knowledge of Scripture, and understanding the problems of society. But what if being one step ahead of the world is *ten thousand steps* behind where God desires to take us?

Imagine if, just as loving parents desire their infant to learn to walk and not continue crawling for the rest of his life, God desired us to learn to *spiritually* walk, then run, then jump, then scale the most difficult mountain passes known to man.

Imagine if, just as loving parents desire their toddler to

gain a vocabulary, God desired us to learn to talk with Him, then listen to Him, then represent Him before the powers and rulers of this earth?

Imagine if, just as loving parents desire their three-year-old to learn to share his toys, God desired us to learn to love and give of ourselves, then sacrifice all our earthly comforts to build His kingdom, then even shed our blood for Him as a statement of the greatest love?

Imagine if there was *so much more* that God had in mind for us than we see modeled in the Christian community today. Imagine if He really did desire us to dream the impossible as little kids and then actually *live* the impossible as adults.

Imagine if our relationship with the God of the Universe was not just a dull religious routine but an *endless frontier* of possibility and adventure.

Unfortunately, today's Christianity breeds settlers rather than pioneers. It has bred men and women who no longer comb the wilds of God's grace. And it's time we realize that knowing Christ is an endless frontier—a frontier into which we have taken but one measly step.

Embarking upon the Adventure

This book is about the art of living. But not just any kind of living. *Christ-enabled living. Impossible living. Heroic living.* It is about the discovery of a life scripted by the Author of true purpose and adventure. If you are willing to awaken your inner pioneer, this book can help you venture into a new and magnificent world.

Of course, this book can't roll up your sleeping bag and

pack up your tent for you. It can't force you out of your comforts and into the untamed endless frontier of a God-scripted life adventure. It can merely function as a map to show you the way.

This book is about exchanging the ordinary human life for the extraordinary life of God. It's not for the faint of heart; it's not for those satisfied with mediocrity; and it's certainly not for those content with playing life at the beginners' level. It's about breaking through impenetrable blockades, scaling impassable barriers, and achieving impossible dreams. It's about learning to play life at the expert level and actually winning.

The world mocks the premise of this book. Even many Christians scornfully shake their heads at this kind of message, denouncing it under the label of "youthful zeal." They say there is no endless frontier to explore, that achieving the impossible is better left up to James Bond and his Hollywood cronies. But the premise of this book is based on the reality of God Himself and on His very words contained in the holy Scriptures: "The things that are impossible with people are possible with God."[6] It's high time we as Christians got back our little-kid hankering for lives that beat insurmountable odds.

The adventure begins with simple faith—being confident that God is who He says He is; realizing that we have only begun to know Him; resting assured that He will reward those who diligently seek Him, and believing that He will be found by those who desire to find Him.

As little kids we trust in the impossible, even to a fault. We fall for make-believe things from the Tooth Fairy to Bigfoot. And we are *certain* that they exist, living our lives as if they are real. It's that same little-kid certainty that we as adults are missing when it comes to believing in the God of the Universe. That is why Jesus Christ says that to enter into His kingdom we first must "become like children."[7] When we approach God with a childlike assurance that He is exactly who He claims to be, the adventure begins and never ends.

So allow your little-kid dreams to be reawakened. Allow the pioneer within you to come alive—that inner spiritual explorer that longs to pursue a bigger-than-life action drama with God. The God of the Universe wants to write your life story. And when He does, you mustn't expect a mediocre tale.

For there is in the mysterious depths
of the Triune God neither limit nor end.[8]
A. W. TOZER

Let us never hesitate to say,
"This is only the beginning."[9]
ANDREW MURRAY

In a Nutshell

God created us as little kids with a passion for impossible things. But He never intended for us to have that passion stripped away as we grew into adulthood. He wants us to believe in Him, the God of the Impossible. He wants us to expect Him to be as large as He says He is and as capable as He claims to be.

God created us for adventure, for pursuit, and for pioneering. His greatness and glory are spread about a vast and endless frontier, as fathomless as the universe itself. And it's into that boundless frontier that He beckons us, "Come and know Me!" It's a lifelong quest of discovery and growth.

As Christians, we are meant to have an insatiable appetite for God, seeking Him as a miner searches for gold, never satisfied with only a small nugget of His beauty but longing to hold the entire treasure of His grace. The gold of God is awaiting discovery. The ultimate life is waiting to be lived. But first we must awaken the pioneer within us. We must, once again, dream impossible dreams.

two

Leslie

PACKING UP OUR TENTS

shaking off the settler mentality

> *My prayer today is that God would make me an*
> *extraordinary Christian.*[10]
> GEORGE WHITEFIELD

What does a God-scripted existence really look like? Sadly, we see very few examples of it in modern Christianity. If we were to be honest, most of us would have to admit that we only imagine a victorious, peaceful, vibrant relationship with Jesus Christ.

Dreaming of Balmy Breezes

Eric and I spent eight years traveling and speaking. That may sound glamorous, but believe me, it wasn't.

I am sure that if you are Sting or Shania, life on the road is a study in luxury and glitz. But spending your flight in a cramped middle seat next to a screaming child, spilling orange juice down the front of your pants, and being yelled at by a grouchy flight attendant on your way to the bathroom definitely keeps the glamour of travel at bay. Life on the road for Eric and me was mostly about jet lag, greasy food, and getting lost.

We have raced across terminals to catch departing flights, spilling boxes of books and brochures in a chaotic heap as other passengers stepped around us. We have been stranded by blizzards in desolate hotels without food. We have performed while green with the stomach flu. And we have appeared onstage in our sweats because the airline sent our luggage to Las Vegas instead of Chicago.

Glamour has never been in the picture for us.

So when Eric and I had an opportunity to go to Hawaii on a romantic getaway two years ago, we jumped at the chance. After years of pulling wrinkled clothes from suitcases and enduring more than our share of embarrassing moments, we knew that a tropical vacation was probably the closest we'd ever get to glamorous travel.

As the date of our departure approached, we were giddy with anticipation. Staring impatiently out the windows of our Colorado home, we saw nothing but icy roads and blowing snow. Longingly, we pictured ourselves on the sunny beaches of Hawaii. We imagined the feeling of warm sand squishing between our toes and the sound of waves crashing gently against the shore. We studied a United States map so that we could better visualize the island of Maui, where we'd soon be slathering on suntan lotion and sipping lemonade.

We had fun dreaming about our trip. But it was no comparison to actually being there. Once we abandoned the winterized terrain of Colorado for the balmy breezes of the islands, we no longer had to imagine what Hawaii was like.

When we finally arrived on the soft sandy beach, we put away our map.

And we experienced it for ourselves.

In Search of Something More

When it comes to the Christian life, most of us are like eager vacationers gearing up for a trip to Maui, dreaming about the warm sand and sunny beaches and studying the island on a map. But though we dream about, talk about, and plan our transition from frigid snowdrifts to summery shores, *we never actually get there.*

What does a God-scripted existence really look like on a day-to-day basis? Sadly, we see very few examples of it in modern Christianity. If we were to be honest, most of us would have to admit that we only *imagine* a victorious, peaceful, vibrant relationship with Jesus Christ.

We hear about the joy, peace, and fulfillment that Christ can bring, and there are moments when we experience glimmers of it, perhaps after hearing a deeply moving message at church or reading an inspirational book.

But the feeling doesn't last.

Life gets in the way and soon our struggles with compromise, depression, anxiety, or bitterness are just as intense as they were before. We study Maui on a map and pretend that we are there, but in actuality we are still dwelling in the desolate tundra of a perpetual winter. We hide our true spiritual lives under a facade called "the Christian game," only dreaming about the endless frontier of a God-written life.

Whatever form it takes, most of us—young and old—are stuck in the Christian game. We've traded passionate, vibrant intimacy with Christ for shallow Christian hype. We've accepted a cheap imitation of the real thing, a worthless cubic zirconium instead of a priceless diamond.

Most of us don't even realize that there is *something more* awaiting us in our earthly lives, something infinitely more sweet and satisfying than we have ever imagined.

When we become trapped in the Christian game, we are too distracted and disillusioned to notice the endless frontier of adventure that is calling to us. We tell ourselves we are pioneers, exploring the depths of a Christ-built life. But in reality we are only settlers studying the pioneer's map in the comfort and safety of our tents.

Jordan is a graceful blonde who is active in her church, has loving Christian parents, and is surrounded by wonderful Christian friends. She is gearing up for her first year at a well-known Christian university. On the outside, her life seems perfect. But Jordan has a shameful secret. She is involved in an ongoing sexual relationship that no one knows about. She is living a secret life of compromise.

"I feel so far away from God right now," she whispered bitterly after explaining her dilemma to me. "I can't seem to stop sinning no matter how much I want to. I have prayed and prayed about this, but God never gives me any answers!

"I really need to know something," Jordan pleaded desperately. "Does Christianity even work, or is it all just a fairy tale?"

Jordan is trapped in the Christian game.

And then there is Trent, a brainy history buff who wrote Eric a lengthy e-mail describing his spiritual struggle. Trent attended a Christian leadership retreat and got extremely excited about pursuing a deeper relationship with Christ. But a few weeks after his return home, the passion faded.

"No matter how hard I try to grow in my walk with Christ," he lamented, "I just don't feel the fire. No matter what I do to stay pumped up spiritually, it just doesn't last." Trent attends church and studies his Bible, but inwardly he wallows in depression and disillusionment.

Trent is trapped in the Christian game.

Hollow Imitations

Before we explore what true Christianity really looks like, let's first examine what it is *not*. In modern Christian circles, we are surrounded by all too many imitation versions of Christianity. The Christian game takes on many different forms, but the end result is the same: *It keeps us comfortable where we are*. The Christian game lulls us to sleep in the comfort of our tents. It keeps us from pursuing the "something more" we inwardly long for.

How many of us have been in Jordan or Trent's position? We *believe* the right things, *say* the right things, and even *do* the right things, only to end up right back where we started: defeated, discouraged, and conquered by sin. We know the truth in theory, but it has no power to really transform our lives at the deepest level. We go through the motions of Christianity while secretly asking ourselves, *Is this all there is?*

We are trapped in the Christian game.

The game leads to an empty form of Christianity. It may make us feel better about ourselves from time to time, but it does not shape us into the real-life action heroes or passionate pioneers that God has called us to become.

Though we may not speak it aloud, many of us often wonder if our mediocre spiritual existence is all there really is to the Christian life. We stare dejectedly out the window at the winterized terrain and begin to wonder if the island of Maui is just an intangible myth, a place to dream about but never personally experience.

Unfortunately, even some Christian leaders try to convince us to remain in the frigid land of apathy and defeat. They tell us we were never meant to discover the something more we are inwardly searching for. They write thought-provoking books and deliver passionate messages explaining that the sunny beaches of Hawaii were only meant to be studied on a map, not actually experienced in person. They chuckle and shake their heads at those who long to trade the icy chill of winter for the warmth of summer shores.

If you are among those in our disillusioned generation who are stubbornly longing for more, we want to let you in on a secret.

Something more does exist. And once you get a taste of the true adventure God has called you to, you will never again be satisfied with merely studying the map.

"Just Be Real" Christianity

Our generation has seen the hypocrisy of make-believe Christianity and, to put it mildly, we don't like it. Thousands of us are saying "*Hasta la vista*" to the playacting version of following God. While earlier generations were prone to super-stiff religiosity and legalistic formulas, many of us in this generation have headed in the opposite direction, determined to *be real* about our emotions, struggles, and failures.

This has led to a common form of imitation Christianity we call "just be real" Christianity. Don't get us wrong. Being real is important. Admitting that we aren't perfect is the first step towards discovering successful Christianity. But it isn't the final goal. *Being real* and finding a *real Christian experience* are two very different things.

Paul, a twenty-three-year-old Bible school student has decided to "be real" about his lustful addictions. "I'm hooked on pornography!" he blurts flippantly. "That's just the way it is. God knows I'm only human, and I'm not gonna beat myself up about it."

Tiffany, an eighteen-year-old Christian, has chosen to be open about her burning anger toward her Creator. "I hate God sometimes," she boldly declares. "I wish I could scream in His face. He's treated me like garbage. And I think it's better to be honest about it than act like everything's fine."

The "just be real" version of Christianity removes the plastic bandage and exposes the infection underneath. But the "just be real" version doesn't allow the wound to be healed; it only acknowledges that the wound exists.

It is vital that we acknowledge the emptiness of the Christian game. But when we settle for the "just be real" version of Christianity, we are still miles away from the true Christian life. We admit defeat, but we never search for victory. We are honest about our problems, but we ignore the solution. We remain trapped in the Christian game.

"God Loves Me Anyway" Christianity

A common accessory to the "just be real" mind-set is the "God Loves Me Anyway" version of imitation Christianity.

The "God loves me anyway" attitude ignores God's command to "BE HOLY, FOR I AM HOLY."[11] It shies away from the sting of conviction. It buries the prick of guilt. And it treats every spiritual challenge that triggers even the slightest emotional discomfort as if it were the first symptom of the bubonic plague. And the pain of sin's havoc upon our soul is alleviated with smooth religious rhetoric.

Kelly grew up in a strict religious home, full of rules but devoid of unconditional love. In college, when Kelly began a serious romantic relationship with a worship leader named Damon, things began to turn around. She felt loved and accepted for the first time in her life.

Though Kelly and Damon had committed to save sex until marriage, one night in the heat of passion, they gave in to temptation. Afterwards, Kelly was plagued with intense guilt. She sat alone in her room for hours, crying with remorse over the mistake she and Damon had made. She knew she had let God down.

But the very next night, she heard a message at church that eased her mind. The pastor seemed to be speaking directly to her. "Christ doesn't condemn us," he declared with conviction. "He loves us just the way we are in all our sin and weakness. God doesn't expect us to be perfect. He knows we are stuck in the mire of our sinfulness. He knows we can't achieve a holy life."

Then the pastor told his listeners to close their eyes and simply receive God's unconditional love. As the worship team played a soft reflective melody, Kelly closed her eyes and felt a sense of relief flood her soul. She repeated the pastor's words that God loved her in spite of her failure, that He didn't expect her to be perfect.

And Kelly's guilt floated away like a cloud.

Since then, Kelly and Damon have maintained an ongoing sexual relationship. Kelly continues to push away any feelings of guilt by listening to inspiring messages about God's unconditional love. She convinces herself that God accepts her in spite of her mistakes and that He doesn't expect her to change.

Kelly, like so many in our disillusioned generation, has pitched her tent in the "God loves me anyway" camp. Though she is enslaved to compromise and defeated by sin, she has given up trying to overcome these obstacles. When it comes to her Christian walk, she doesn't even consider exploring the endless frontier of God's ways. She spends her energy reminding herself that God loves her in the midst of her miserable-but-forgiven state. And she has given up expecting anything more.

It's important to note that there is a thread of truth woven into the false foundation of the "God loves me anyway" attitude. It is true that God knows our sinful condition and loves us in spite of our failures. He is not looking down at us with angry eyes, burning with fury every time we make a mistake. He loves us more than we could ever comprehend.

But He loves us too much to leave us as we are.

Sin is the great hindrance to our relationship with God. Sin—the self-reliance and self-assurance at the core of our beings—is the very thing Jesus Christ came to this earth to conquer. And as long as this selfish rule is the controlling force within our souls, His mighty work on the cross two thousand years ago is rendered ineffective in our lives. While sin remains the ruler of our inner domain, we can never experience the true Christian life.

If we settle for the "God loves me anyway" approach to life, we will never experience more than a shallow, mediocre spiritual existence. We will remain under the thumb of sin's tyranny, trying to cover up our remorse with T-shirts that say, "I'm not perfect, I'm just forgiven."

God did not send His only Son to conquer sin and death on our behalf just so we could wallow in defeat and compromise while singing songs about His unconditional love. Jesus Christ died to give us *true* life—a life marked by a radiance and righteousness that transforms our entire existence.

"Professional Christianity"

Another modern pitfall is what could be called "Professional Christianity."

Meet Mason, a twenty-eight-year-old seminary graduate currently in search of a full-time pastoral position at a church. Mason knows Scripture better than most people know their own name. He believes all the right doctrinal truths. He even stands out to his non-Christian friends as a solid, moral guy who doesn't drink, do drugs, or sleep around.

But Mason's Christian life is hollow and self-constructed. There is nothing miraculous or supernatural about his spiritual existence. His aim in life isn't to climb God's holy mountain, but merely to live a life that is morally superior to those around him. He believes that God's expectations for his life equate to a little hill that can easily be tackled with some discipline and willpower.

Mason smirks at the concept of a God-written life. "God doesn't waste His time watching over us like a momma bear. He has better things to do. He doesn't care about the details of our lives. He just wants us to live morally and make good decisions."

Mason has pitched his tent in the "professional Christianity" realm. He has traded in the possibility of a radical pursuit of Christ for a predictable moral existence. He has baked Christianity down to a formula he can easily accomplish in his own strength.

All too many of us fall into the "professional Christianity" trap. We separate God from the details of our daily lives. We reduce our Christian walk to a set of reasonable guidelines to follow. We remove all the risk, passion, and radical obedience from our spiritual life.

And we revel over the points we've scored in the Christian game.

Putting the Game Away

God's expectations for our lives go far beyond these imitation forms of following Him. The only way we can begin the adventure He has called us to is by putting away the Christian game. We must recognize that we are covered in the sludge of mediocrity. We must admit that we have been drugged into a slumberous state of comfort and predictability. We must choose to leave behind our hollow imitation versions of Christianity and boldly venture into the breathtaking expanse of God's love and grace.

Oswald Chambers, whose teachings were compiled into the well-known devotional *My Utmost for His Highest,* candidly described his departure from the Christian game:

I was doing Christian work and winning souls for Christ…but I had no conscious communion with Him. The Bible was the dullest, most uninteresting book in existence. I knew that if what I had was all the Christianity there was, the whole thing was a fraud.

During a Christian gathering, Chambers stood up and admitted before the group that he was in desperate need of a true encounter with the King of all kings. He finally came to grips with the fact that all of his Christian training, spiritual leadership, and religious activities did not amount to a passionate relationship with Jesus Christ.[12]

For Oswald Chambers, acknowledging the emptiness of the Christian game was the first step into a vibrant, victorious Christian life that impacted millions. He had to come to the end of himself, recognize his own inability to make true Christianity work, and begin his pursuit of something more.

In order to experience a God-scripted life, we too must put aside our spiritual pretenses. We must come face-to-face with our desperate need for something more. We must choose not to settle for the apathy of the Christian game.

The life God has planned for us is not something we can accomplish in our own strength. Later, we will discuss the secret that enables us to live a vibrant and victorious Christian existence. But it all starts here—with shaking off our settler mentality and packing up our tents in pursuit of something more and recognizing that our self-built, imitation versions of Christianity cannot replace a passionate relationship with the King of kings.

Putting It into Action

It's hard for us to admit when we are wrong. And it's especially hard for us to admit that we have bought into a cheap imitation of the true Christian life. But that's where the God-scripted adventure begins. Before a settler can be transformed into a pioneer, he must first become dissatisfied with his current surroundings. He must recognize his need for something better.

If you are ready to begin your pursuit into God's endless frontier, take some time to ask yourself these soul-searching questions:

- When it comes to knowing Christ, have I stopped growing and pitched my tent? Have I bought into an imitation version of following God?
- Have I settled for a "just be real" mind-set, admitting that I have problems but not believing that God can grant me victory over them?
- Have I settled for a "God loves me anyway" attitude, taking sin lightly and letting selfishness, rather than righteousness, rule my life?
- Have I settled for "professional Christianity," reducing God's expectations for my life to a set of reasonable guidelines I can hope to accomplish on my own?

Be completely honest as you ask yourself these questions. Don't compare your life to those of Christians around you. Let Jesus Christ be your only standard. And as God begins to show you areas of your spiritual life that are off track, put these in writing and make a commitment to shift from settler to pioneer in these areas.

When we are willing to acknowledge the shallow emptiness of our self-made spiritual lives and ask God to carry us into the endless frontier of knowing Him, we open the door to a journey of discovery beyond anything we've ever dreamed.

And once we embark on the pioneer's journey, we will quickly realize that the adventure has only just begun.

It is not what a man achieves,
but what he believes and strives
for that makes him noble and great. [13]

OSWALD CHAMBERS

In a Nutshell

God created us to experience vibrant daily intimacy with Him and to constantly pursue even greater depths of relationship with Him. But too often, once we scratch the surface of knowing Him, we pitch our tent. We stop pursuing Him. We stop seeking Him. And instead of having a daily, passionate relationship with our God, we settle for an imitation. We become trapped in the shallowness of the Christian game. We sing songs about His love and read books about His grace, but we rarely experience Him in our daily lives.

To experience the something more that each of us longs for, we must put away the Christian game, reject our imitation versions of Christianity, pack up our tents, and embark upon the adventure of truly knowing God. We must shake off the settler's mentality and become pioneers, passionately pursuing more and more of our King.

three

Eric

MOUNT EVEREST CHRISTIANITY

knowing our true destination

> *If only He had told us to hitch our wagon to a mule, we could see how it might be done; but to tell us to hitch our natural lumbering wagons to the star of Almighty God makes us wonder whether we have understood Him aright.*[14]
>
> OSWALD CHAMBERS

We have long aimed our lives at climbing spiritual molehills, but God commands more of us. His Holy Everest is meant to be the aim and the prize of every Christian life—the destination of every soul that loves God and desires to experience the depths of His love.

Standing Next to Greatness

I once met the World's Strongest Man.

I was nineteen and home from college on Christmas break when my brother received a flyer from his church youth group announcing an upcoming special appearance by "Mr. Massive." I could hardly contain myself. If there was one thing I respected at the energetic age of nineteen, it was gargantuan muscles. Maybe it's because mine were so puny.

That Sunday morning I snuck into my brother's class to have a peek at this amazing hulk of a man. Rumor had it that he could bench-press over seven hundred pounds!

I'll never forget approaching him after his brief talk ended. While he was signing a picture of himself for some wide-eyed high-school guy, I just stared at his bulging biceps in awe.

Whoa! I thought. *His arms are as big around as my waist!*

"Hi there," Mr. Massive said in my direction, startling me from my reverie. "What's your name?"

"Uh, Eric L-l-ludy!" I said with a tremor in my voice as I shook his dinosaur paw of a hand. His neck was the size of a barrel—it would have taken six of my hands to strangle him. His chest could have doubled for the Rock of Gibraltar.

When I finally found my voice, I asked him some idiotic question about how I could exchange my skinny body for a massive one like his. It was one of those questions that you ponder over and over for days afterwards and think, *That was so stupid!*

What I remember about that day, other than my stupidity, is how small I was next to Mr. Massive. He could have packed five Eric Ludys into his frame and still had plenty of room left over.

I had been working hard myself to become the ultimate physical specimen. I lifted weights every day, ran mile after mile, drank protein drinks the way an elephant imbibes water, scarfed down four plates of college cafeteria food every night, and flexed in front of the mirror daily to check my progress. I actually thought I was getting somewhere until I came face-to-face with *him*. Mr. Massive.

When I was nineteen, I witnessed the spectacle of this mountain of muscle and felt the uncomfortable twinge of realizing my own smallness. I saw up close how physically imposing and powerful a human being could actually become. And as a result, I saw how skinny and weak I really was.

But it was only a few months later when I encountered something much more impressive and more important than a man's muscles. It was then that I first came face-to-face with how big my God is.

The Ultimate Destination

Stand me next to the world's strongest man and, sure, I look dwarfish by comparison. But stand our scrawny Christian lives next to the triumphant, all-loving, perfectly holy life of Jesus Christ, and it's like standing a Coke bottle next to the Empire State Building.

You might have thought I was crazy, at the age of nineteen, to think that I could take my scrawny body and transform it into something akin to Mr. Massive's physique. But how much more crazy do I seem now, at the age of thirty-three, when I declare that it is my desire to see this pitiful little life of Eric Ludy transformed into the very image of Jesus Christ?

I no longer care about leaping over tall buildings in a single bound or lifting semitrucks with one hand. Those were childish longings, little-kid passions not yet harnessed and directed by the Spirit of God and made ready for the real world.

Yes, I did go through my phase of wanting the world's

biggest muscles. There was even a time when I longed to be *People* magazine's "Sexiest Man Alive." (No laughter, please!) But those were misguided dreams, not yet matured and shaped around the person of Jesus Christ.

I dream larger now than ever before. I don't care to be an Einstein, a Cicero, a Sinatra, or an Elway. I now long to be a replica of the heroic life of Jesus Christ.

What I yearn for now is greater than the composite of all the great Marvel Comics superheroes rolled into one: *I desire to have the superconquering King of the Universe make my body His earthly palace.* I dream of being forged into His very likeness, showcasing to the world what God can do through a life fully submitted to Him. I dream of allowing the God of the impossible to truly *live out* the impossible in and through my being.

I've aimed my life in the direction of the highest peak—a destination beyond even Mount Everest. It's God's Holy Everest that I dream of climbing.

But this isn't just my dream. This is the impossible dream He wants every one of His children to dream.

The first thing necessary for any adventure is a destination. We each must choose which direction our life will take and toward what end we are headed. For many years now, we Christians have obsessed over climbing spiritual molehills, when God commands us to aim much higher. We have chosen a direction that leads to the doldrums of spiritual mediocrity and prohibits us from ever entering the endless frontiers of Christ's grace.

God's Holy Everest is meant to be the aim and the prize of every Christian life—the destination of every soul that loves God and desires to experience the depths of His love.

Unfortunately, God's Everest is unfamiliar territory to

many of us. Most of us never realize there is more to Christianity than attending church and putting 10 percent of our income into the offering plate each week. So let's pause a moment and take a closer look at this holy and grand destination God has in mind for us.

Viewing Everest

The following is a humble attempt to offer a brief glimpse of the endless possibilities of the Christian life. To describe such a glorious mountain is like trying to describe heaven itself. Please know that the true dimension of potentiality is beyond my human understanding and my limited experience. Please forgive me for merely scratching the surface of the amazing wonder of a life shared with the Creator of the Universe.

Imagine responding to life's trials like Cheerios in milk—totally unsinkable. No matter what is thrown at you, you bob right back up to the surface with an enormous smile. Whether you are tortured, imprisoned, or even robbed of life itself, you respond with perfect peace and unwavering joy.

Imagine your soul blazing with the passionate fire of God. You possess an unearthly confidence that strikes fear into anyone who opposes the Truth you stand for. You have nothing to lose, because you have already lost everything. To you, suffering for Christ is the highest honor, the ultimate opportunity to express your adoration and devotion to Him.

Imagine never having to seek human comfort and ease. Rather, you long to be broken bread and poured-out wine for your majestic Lover and Lord. You don't strive for the approval of men, but live for the applause of your King alone. You aren't driven by ordinary human ambition; you are driven by God-built ambition. You wait for the command of your Master and Commander, and you instantly obey Him with delight, no matter the degree of difficulty or challenge of the given task.

Imagine God being near to you, every moment of the day. To you, Jesus Christ is not just a historical figure found in the pages of the Bible, but real and dear, an intimate Lover, sharing every waking moment of your life with you. His touch upon your heart is the purest delight. His voice is more familiar to you than your closest friend's, and the scent of His presence wafts through your inner being like sweet perfume. To you, worship is never-ending. Your heart and mind stand in awe of the infinite beauty and grandeur of almighty God.

Imagine being unconcerned with superficial things. You don't worry about clothes, food, relationships, or money. You are captivated by Jesus Christ, and everything else fades into oblivion. To you, heaven is far more real than your earthly life. Worshiping your Prince for all eternity is your greatest desire.

Imagine winning battles over sin daily. You are not overcome by temptation's slithery enticement. You find supernatural power to fight for personal righteousness. Every successful battle fortifies you and makes you stronger. Your life is a radiant reflection of Jesus Christ. You have adopted His holiness as your very own.

Imagine your life as the most pure and perfect demonstration of God's nature this world could ever see. You love like He loves, serve like He serves, and overcome like He overcomes. Your life story is a divine triumph that continues throughout eternity.

Okay, Let's Get Real

How many of us can honestly say that this vision describes our experience with Jesus Christ?

Some of us might try to respond with the "spiritual" answer: "Well, [cough] of course, I am experiencing that! [Clear throat] I mean, if that's what God intended, then yes, that's exactly what I have found in my Christian walk. Praise the Lord!"

Or if we are part of the "just be real" crowd, we might scoff. "That's so outrageously ridiculous! That's not even remotely close to reality. It's impossible to live that way!"

When we come face-to-face with the life that God has called us to, we must either deny or embrace it. We must either explain it away or, like a little child, trust that God says what He means and means what He says.

The "just be real" Christian looks at the outrageous heights of God's Everest and just laughs at the idea of ever scaling it. On the other hand, the "Professional Christian" mind-set grooms us to treat God's Holy Everest like a mole-hill we can conquer in our own strength. But as long as we continue playing the Christian game, we will never begin to climb to the holy heights God has called us to.

God never meant for us to pitch our tents at the base of His mighty mountain and only talk about climbing it. He means for us to *actually experience* a vibrant, victorious Christian existence. He intends for us to climb His Holy Everest, and in so doing, enter into the boundless exploration of the endless frontiers of His grace.

Futile Attempts at Perfection

When I first learned that God desired me to reach the top of His holy mountain, I immediately attempted to venture its difficult terrain and scale the steep mountain face on my own. This is an all-too-common reaction to the impossible call of God.

I was passionate for God and wanted to please Him, so I gritted my teeth and began my journey. The problem was, I couldn't seem to get very far. Every time I began the trek, I found myself slipping in the mud of compromise and getting overturned and rerouted by the white-water rapids of selfishness. Instead of scaling triumphantly up the steep mountainside of God's holy expectations, I found myself losing my handhold on the rocky face and falling headlong down the entire distance I had just climbed. Every time, I landed with a thud on an outcropping called "Nice try."

I thought that everything in life was all about hard work and effort. I recalled the words of my vocal coach: "Eric, if you want to be the best singer, you have to practice six hours every day." I figured Christianity must be the same. If I just dug down deep, disciplined my life, and tried my hardest, surely good things would come.

After all, when it came to singing, my hard work showed results. When it came to physical endurance, my running routine showed that consistency was the key. But in my Christian walk, my discipline wasn't transforming me into the perfect and pure picture of Jesus Christ I so desperately wanted to be.

As the years passed, I tried everything to overcome my spiritual limitations and somehow climb God's Holy Everest. I read my Bible for hours on end. I woke myself up at two in the morning to pray. I fasted for long periods of time, hoping that my physical suffering would equal spiritual strength. I went on multiple missions trips, sacrificing my own comforts to serve others. I even gave away my financial and material resources, hoping to find the secret of spiritual success. But no matter what I tried, I was attempting to climb an impossible mountain face, slipping every time.

The Long Heavy Object

As a man, this is an embarrassing story to tell. When the events of this story were unfolding, I was nineteen, still yet to meet Mr. Massive and still sadly and humorously very much enamored with my muscular strength. It was moving day for my friend's cousin's aunt. And somehow I got roped into helping.

I don't remember what the object was, but it was oblong and super heavy. And it needed to be carried to the fifth floor of an apartment building in Denver.

"It looks like you'll need a hand with that one," one of the guys said.

I interpreted his statement to mean, "Eric, there is no way that you could possibly move that piece by yourself." I stiffened up at his suggestion and coolly responded, "I've got it!"

"Okay." He shrugged. "Just holler if you need me."

With that, he picked up a box from the U-Haul and began his journey up five long flights of stairs.

I gritted my teeth and lifted the awkward item, determined to transport the long heavy object in record time and prove my buddy wrong.

Thirty-six minutes later I found myself on the landing at the top of the first flight of stairs. I still had four stories to go.

My body was in utter agony. My shins were scraped raw, my hands were in terrible pain, and I was jammed into a corner and couldn't move.

"Still got it?" My friend smirked as he jumped over the railing to get by my roadblock.

"Uh, I think I could use a little help," I muttered with an unstable voice.

"A *little* help? Admit it, man, you need a *lot* of help!"

In Need of a Lot of Help

As Christians, our goal is none other than to become a perfect mirrorlike reflection of Jesus Christ. So we dig down deep, grit our teeth, and heave, attempting to move the super-heavy expectations of God up innumerable flights of stairs without any help. We try—and we are met with certain failure.

The whole while, Jesus Christ is standing near, just waiting for us to acknowledge our inability to achieve perfection. "It looks as if you are going to need a hand with that," He kindly offers, knowing that our self-determination is hindering us from realizing the impossibility of the task.

"I've got it!" we confidently reply.

With a knowing glance, He gently says, "Just holler when you need Me."

For some of us, the impossible journey up the stairs is short-lived; we realize our weakness quickly and admit that we need assistance. But many of us attempt to impress God with our strength and resolve, wanting to show Him our love by trying to do what He already knows we can't. Eventually, we grow exhausted and falter. And amidst that human failure we hear His tender voice saying, "Are you ready for Me to step in now?"

God doesn't mind us attempting to pull off the impossible. In fact, He knows that to truly understand our need for Him, we must try and carry the impossible weight—we must try and scale His Everest. He knows that human failure leads us to recognize our gigantic need for assistance. In His great love for us, He allows us to try, and He also allows us to fail. Because only then are we finally ready to embrace the only solution to the problem: *God Himself*.

The Bible says that the "law was our schoolmaster to bring us unto Christ."[15] God's law was given to Moses as the representation of Jesus Christ's perfection and holiness. Attempting to follow that law leads us to the realization that we simply cannot do it in our own strength and discipline. This experience reveals to us that we desperately need a Helper. It proves to our heart and mind that we need a Rescuer. It shows us that we need Jesus Christ Himself if we are ever going to follow in His perfect footsteps.

God wants us to dream impossible dreams, and He never wants us to stop short of seeing them become reality. But along the way, He will teach us that the impossible is only made possible by Him. Human effort will never get us to the great heroic destination of God. But if we beckon the God of the Impossible to take over and rescue our hapless lives, then the frontiers of Christlikeness can become a vibrant reality.

Putting It into Action

Set your course for Christ. Trust that He means what He says when He states, "You are to be perfect, as your heavenly

Father is perfect."[16] And trust that though you can't personally muster the power to achieve His expectations, *He can* get you up that mountain.

1. Pursue the Impossible

Even though you are incapable of climbing His Everest, *He is capable*. And even though the rarified air of holiness is humanly impossible for us to breathe, it is air that He is very much accustomed to, having breathed it every moment throughout all eternity. And He is a God that is fully capable of working the impossible in and through our lives. We simply must set our course for Christ, calibrate our compass around His expectations, and allow Him to carry us, as He Himself scales the majestic mountains with us firmly in His grasp. Sure, we can't trek this mountain on our own; but if we have Him, we can conquer its impossible terrain. We must dream the impossible dream that He Himself dreams for our lives.

2. Lose Faith in Yourself

The key to the Christian life is faith—an implicit trust that God is who He says He is, has done what He says He has done, and can do what He says He can do. Faith is the entry point into God's kingdom as well as the fuel for an ever-growing spiritual bonfire blazing within our souls. Faith in God's ability is the catalyst to the God-written life, while faith in our own ability is the ultimate blockade to Christian growth.

Many of us are confident in ourselves. We feel, if given

the chance, we can prove our quality and scale God's Everest on our own. But as long as we have faith in ourselves, we can't have faith in God. So ask God to help you lose confidence in your own ability to imitate Him. Allow Him to prove to you in no uncertain way that you are totally and completely unable to scale His Everest. And request that He show you how desperately you need a Savior and a Helper to complete His course. The sooner you stop trusting in your own ability, the sooner God will be able to begin working in and through your life.

3. Allow Yourself to Be Carried

As long as we try on our own to scale God's impossible expectations, we will fail, because the only way up the steep slopes of God's Everest is to be carried up in His strong arms. But very few of us are willing to humble ourselves and admit that we must be carried. Being carried is the ultimate sign of dependence. Being carried means someone else controls the course of my life. But being carried also means we have faith that Someone other than ourselves is capable of doing for us what we could never accomplish on our own.

To be carried, we simply must ask. We simply must believe that what is impossible with man is possible with God. We must humble ourselves and crawl up into His strong arms and rest our entire weight upon Him. A life carried by God is a life written by God. To cry out to God and say, "Lord, please carry me!" is the entrance into Christ's most intimate and glorious chamber of delight.

For I, through attempting to carry out God's holy expectations, have come to my end and lost faith in myself that I might now live unto God. I am crucified with Christ: nevertheless I live; yet not I, but Christ liveth in me: and the life which I now live in the body I live by faith in the Son of God, who loved me, and gave himself for me.[17]

THE APOSTLE PAUL

In a Nutshell

To enter the endless frontier of a God-scripted life, we must gain a clear picture of our true destination. As modern Christians, we often aim our lives at the wrong targets. We aim to climb molehills and splash around in wading pools when God destined us to climb majestic mountain peaks and ford mighty oceans. God intends for us to scale the impassable mountainside of His holiness. He has called us to follow in the footsteps of Jesus Christ—a path no human being has ever been able to muster up the willpower or discipline to do. God crafted us to reach a destination in our lives that we are humanly unable to reach.

We must come face-to-face with our utter inability to take even one step into this endless frontier on our own. God desires to lift us up with His strong arms, take complete control of our lives, and tackle the rugged mountainous terrain on our behalf, while we lean our entire weight upon His solid chest. Without Him, we can do nothing.

four

Leslie

HOLY MOMENTUM

carried upstream by the mighty current of Christ

> *Jesus Christ does not want to be our helper;*
> *He wants to be our Life. He does not want us to work for*
> *Him. He want us to let Him do His work through us,*
> *using us as we use a pencil to write with.*[18]
>
> CHARLES TRUMBULL

Can we really achieve lifelong victory in our Christian experience? Is it really possible to reach the peaks of Mount Everest Christianity in our lifetime? It seems like such a far-fetched idea. And yet, most of us long for the something more that the great men and women of God discovered in ages past.

The Crisis

Seven years ago, Eric and I experienced a spiritual crisis in our lives.

It was late one night at a sleepy Wisconsin Denny's, and Eric and I were picking at our cold eggs and hash browns, trying to unwind after a full day of speaking. That's when it came to the surface.

"There's got to be more to the Christian life than this," I blurted, feeling an inner heaviness unlike anything I'd ever known.

Eric just nodded. He was experiencing the same sense of discouragement.

We had just spent the entire day sharing God's Truth with young people. But inwardly we had been battling disillusionment and emptiness for weeks, and it was only growing. Our ministry was thriving, but something in our spiritual life just wasn't working.

Eric and I had been Christians since we were young children. We both grew up in Christian homes. We had an amazing, beautiful, God-written romance. Early in our marriage, we had launched into full-time ministry as energetic young Christians eager to share the Truth with our generation. We were passionate, buoyant, and excited about life.

But after two years of intense full-time ministry, something changed.

Like so many other Christian leaders, we began to feel the weight of financial pressure, exhaustion from travel, and the constant pull of urgent tasks needing our attention. We learned to mask our frustration, anxiety, and discouragement behind sincere-looking smiles and motivational messages. But inside, our spiritual life was shriveling. We got so busy doing "work for Christ" that we lost sight of what had brought us to Him in the first place. We were bogged down in the sludge of the Christian game.

Earlier in life, when our relationship with Christ was new and fresh, we had experienced a vibrant Christian existence. But now we began to wonder if that had just been our youthful zeal and idealism. Now that we had adult-sized trials and responsibilities, we found that we could no longer make victorious Christianity really work in our lives.

Where was the triumphant Christian life that we read about in the New Testament? Where was the dauntless passion for Jesus Christ that the heroes of the faith had experienced? How could we ever hope to reach the peaks of Mount Everest Christianity when we could barely find enough strength to make it through the day?

These questions led us on a spiritual search that would radically alter our lives.

The Search

Just a few weeks later we began to unearth stories of historical Christians that offered us a glimmer of hope. First we came across the story of Hudson Taylor, a pioneer missionary to China in the late 1800s. Even after years of risking his life to serve Jesus Christ and spread the hope of the gospel, Hudson continually struggled with a defeated spiritual existence.

"I mourn that I am so slow to imitate my precious Master," he wrote in a letter to his mother. "I cannot tell you how I am buffeted sometimes by temptation. I never knew how bad a heart I had."

And then Taylor discovered something that transformed his existence. He went from dejected and defeated to victorious and vibrant. And this was not just a passing experience—it lasted for the rest of his life.

"My work was never so plentiful, so responsible, or so difficult as it is now, but the weight and strain I used to feel are gone," Taylor wrote in a joyful letter to his sister. "I long to tell you what the Lord has done for my soul…once I was blind, now I see."

Hudson Taylor had found the secret to a God-scripted adventure. And throughout the rest of his life, which was full of intense challenges and hardships, his joy and peace in Christ never wavered.

A fellow missionary once described Taylor's existence years after his life-altering change. "Here was a man sixty years of age, bearing tremendous burdens, yet absolutely unruffled. Christ was his reason for peace, his power for calm."[19]

As Eric and I read this story, a deep hunger stirred within us. We longed to personally encounter the very same secret that had made Hudson Taylor's spiritual life shine, even in the midst of trials and valleys.

Then we read the story of D. L. Moody, the evangelist who began a powerful ministry in Chicago in the late 1800s. In the early years of his ministry, he was a "dynamo of feverish activity and apparent effectiveness," yet deep in his heart, there was a "dissatisfaction that increased to the point of desperation."

Eric and I could certainly relate to his desperation. Our ministry seemed effective, and we had filled our lives with a frenzy of Christian activities, but internally we felt empty and far away from Christ.

One day, Moody discovered the secret to a God-scripted life. And his spiritual existence was forever altered.

"It is almost too sacred an experience to describe," wrote Moody later. "I can only say that God revealed Himself to me, and I had such an experience of His love that I had to ask Him to hold back His blessing."

From that point on, Moody's ministry was filled with supernatural power, and his personal fire for Christ never went out. Moody described the change in his ministry: "My sermons were not any different; I did not present any new truths, and yet hundreds were converted. I would not go back to where I was before, even if you should give me all the world."

Moody had discovered a Christianity that *worked*, and Eric and I hungered to experience the same thing. We wanted our lives to radiate with holy power, too.[20]

But could we really achieve the same kind of lifelong victory that D. L. Moody and Hudson Taylor had discovered? We had not seen any modern-day examples of Christians who lived in unwavering joy and peace. Maybe it wasn't really possible. And yet our souls longed for the *something more* that these great men of God had found.

With even greater fervor, we continued to search for more stories of historical Christians who had discovered the secret to a vibrant Christian life, and we were amazed at what we found. We read about the life of John Bunyan, who wrote the classic *The Pilgrim's Progress*. We studied the journey of Oswald Chambers, the author of the well-known devotional *My Utmost for His Highest*. We were inspired by the testimony of Andrew Murray, a prolific writer of Christian books, including *Abide in Christ*. We learned about the experiences of Amy Carmichael, a lifelong missionary to India.

All of them shared a common bond.

All of them reached a point in their Christian lives where they became deeply discouraged and defeated. They cried out to God for answers, and they discovered the secret to a vibrant Christian existence. They each encountered the very thing we were desperately longing for.

The Secret

So how did this amazing transformation happen for these men and women of God? Just what *is* the secret to a victorious Christian life that each of them discovered?

It was an exchange.

An exchange of the most dramatic and life-altering proportions.

They gave up their very lives in exchange for the very life of God. They allowed their bodies to be taken over, like a town surrendering to the invasion of a foreign power. They allowed their being to be possessed by a Spirit so holy, so pure, so righteous, that any remnant of selfish sin was burned away in the fire of God's perfect presence. They relinquished complete and total control of their lives to their King, for Him to dispose of as He saw fit. They invited the most divine Guest into the center of their existence and said, "Make this humble stable your princely palace, O holy Lord!"

They each made an exchange. An exchange so pronounced that all heaven stood and cheered as these simple men and women took the very first step up the impossible slopes of God's Everest.

They exchanged life as they knew it for life as God knew it should be.

They exchanged the right to do with their bodies however they saw fit for the life of a servant who only does what the Master requests.

They exchanged their dreams and ambitions for God's great and dramatic plan for their lives.

They exchanged a life ruled and controlled by sin for a life victorious over sin, clothed with joy and triumph.

Such is the secret of every great man and woman of God.

It's the solemn exchange of a humble human life for His majestic holy life.

This is the key to climbing the Holy Everest that God has set before each of us. It is the key that unlocks the impossible life. It is the key that opens the treasure chest of God's limitless grace, with which He transforms our lives into heroic representations of Himself.

Paul described this exchange with a poetry and passion that has stirred the hearts of God's pioneers for centuries: "It is no longer I who live, but Christ lives in me."[21]

Making the Exchange

Walter Wilson was a respected Christian physician in the early 1900s. Several years into his Christian walk, Wilson became severely discouraged. There was no power or victory in his life. He had no sense of God's presence. He didn't feel that his work or ministry was producing any significant results. His Christianity was hollow and empty.

One night, Wilson was deeply challenged by a message he heard at a church service, and he realized that he had been missing the very essence of the true Christian life. He went home, locked himself in his study, and fell on his face before God.

"My Lord," he said brokenly, "I have mistreated You all my life. I have treated You like a servant. When I wanted You, I called for You; when I was about to engage in something important, I beckoned You to come and help me perform my task. I have sought to use You only as a servant to help me in my self-appointed work. I will do so no more."

Then Walter Wilson made the exchange that altered his

existence forever: He traded his own life for the life of Jesus Christ.

> Lord, I give You this body of mine; from my head to my feet, I give it to You. My hands, my limbs, my eyes, my brain; all that I am inside and out, I hand over to You. Live in and through me whatever life You please. You may send this body to Africa, or lay it on a bed with cancer. You may blind my eyes, or send me with Your message to Tibet. You may take this body to the Eskimos, or send it to a hospital with pneumonia. This body of mine is Yours alone from this moment on.[22]

That night, Walter Wilson stepped into the endless frontier of a God-scripted life adventure—and never looked back. His life went from mediocre and meaningless to radical and radiant. Once he exchanged his life for Christ's, Wilson held the secret to a victorious Christian existence. And nothing was ever the same.

From Hudson Taylor to Oswald Chambers, all of the great historical Christians discovered this secret to the true Christian life. They exchanged their own lives for the life of Jesus Christ. They allowed their bodies to be completely overtaken by a foreign power—the very Spirit of almighty God. They no longer lived, but *Christ lived in them*.

Under New Ownership

It sounds like a wonderful concept. But most of us stand in the way of letting Christ truly live in and through us. Instead of giving Him the ownership papers to our home—our body and soul—we treat Him like a hired servant.

We come to Him when we need answers. We expect Him to provide us with quick solutions to our problems. We demand that He meet our needs and follow our self-made agendas. And when He doesn't respond, we quickly dismiss Him and take matters into our own hands. We are led by our own whims and desires. We make our own choices and then ask God to bless them.

A young basketball player named Kyle recently told us, "I've narrowed my college choices down to two different schools that both have great athletic programs. But I can't decide which one to go to. I've prayed about it, but God doesn't answer. Why isn't He helping me with this?"

A spunky college student named Melanie shared a similar problem with us. "I am interested in a wonderful Christian guy, but he seems more attracted to my best friend than to me. For a few months, I've been praying that God would change the situation, but nothing seems to be happening. Why isn't God answering me?"

So many of us fall into the trap that Kyle and Melanie are in. We believe we are submitted to God's will, but in reality we expect Him to bend to our own agenda. We follow our own heart and desires and then ask God to make our spiritual life vibrant in the midst of it all.

But the true Christian life doesn't work that way. When we exchange our life for Christ's, we lay our agendas, dreams, desires, and plans at His feet. We get completely out of the way and allow Him to live His Life through us in whatever way He chooses.

This is a difficult life change to make. For our entire lives, we have been the sole rulers of our internal home. We are used to making the decisions. We are used to calling the shots. But now we must take a lower position.

Our entire home—body, mind, and soul—now belongs to a *new* ruler. We turn the ownership papers over to a *new* Master. He is not *our* servant; we are *His* servant. We come and go as *He* commands.

Even after two years in ministry, Eric and I were amazed to discover how much of our lives were still under *our* control. We had been trying to overcome spiritual struggles using our own strength and willpower. Our joy and peace were conditional upon our circumstances. And as a result, our Christianity mirrored the defeated, mediocre spiritual existence of our modern times.

Before we were married, we had given God the pen to write our love story. But now we knew we must allow Him to write our *life* story. We must give up our existence, so that Christ could live through us.

And once we exchanged our life for His, things began to dramatically change.

We began allowing the still, small whisper of God's Spirit to direct our steps, rather than relying on our own logic and human reasoning. The supernatural power of God's Spirit began challenging and fortifying us to conquer sin and live lives that radiantly reflected the righteousness of Christ. And though that refining fire was painful, we gained the unquenchable joy that comes from a cleansed inner life.

When we turned our ownership papers over to Jesus Christ and allowed our bodies and souls to be occupied by His Spirit, we began our spiritual trek toward Mount Everest Christianity. And now each day when we awake, we experience the unmatched thrill of a God-scripted adventure.

Do we still have struggles? Of course! But our struggles

no longer overcome us. Do we still sin? Of course! But sin no longer controls our lives. A holy Power now rules our souls, and that Power gives us the strength to be "more than conquerors"[23] in every circumstance we face.

The boundless adventure of a God-scripted life is within our reach when we finally recognize that *we can't* but *He can*.

Putting It into Action

For Walter Wilson it was a simple prayer, offering his entire being to the Spirit of Jesus Christ: "Lord, I give You this body of mine, from my head to my feet, I give it to You. All that I am inside and out, I hand over to You. Live in and through me whatever life You please."[24]

For Hudson Taylor it was a focused decision to remove his own control over his life and fully submit to the rule of his faithful Lord. "I am no longer anxious about anything," he wrote, "as I realize that He is able to carry out His will, and His will is mine. It makes no matter where He places me, or how. That is for Him to consider rather than me; for in the easiest positions He will give me His grace, and in the most difficult His grace is sufficient."[25]

For Oswald Chambers it was a moment of implicit obedience. He publicly declared that his own Christianity was a fraud and asked God's Spirit to overtake his entire being. "When you know what God has done for you," he wrote later, "the power and the tyranny of sin is gone, and is replaced with the radiant, unspeakable joy of Christ dwelling within you."[26]

Whatever form it takes, a whispered prayer or a public declaration, exchanging our life for His means forgoing our own agenda and inviting Him to overtake our being. Instead of ruling over our own body, mind, and soul, we become a servant who bows to the commands of a new Ruler. We turn our ownership papers over to a new Master. We allow Him to live through us whatever life He chooses. This is not a decision to be made lightly. When we exchange our life for His, we give up all control.

If you are ready to begin your trek toward the Mount Everest Christianity that God has called us to, ask God to show you what must be done in your heart and mind to exchange your life for His.

The mystery which hath been hid from ages and from generations, but now is made manifest to his saints... is Christ in you, the hope of glory.[27]

THE APOSTLE PAUL

In a Nutshell

A truly heroic existence is made possible through the exchange of my life for God's. When I relinquish the rights to my own body and give them without condition to my heavenly Lord, His Spirit takes up residence within my physical being. *He takes over.* As the apostle Paul said, "It is no longer I who live, but Christ lives in me." Christ becomes King over my life, calling my earthly body His royal palace, His ruling throne. Without this exchange, the Christian life is merely a game, a self-constructed and miserable counterfeit of something vibrant and real.

The Holy Mount Everest God has called us to climb is truly an impossible feat. And success will only come when we recognize that we can't, but that He can. Only when we learn to yield to the power of *Christ in us* can we achieve true victory. We must let go of our existence as we now know it, forgo our own dreams, and get caught up in the dreams of God. We must exchange our life for His.

part two

LIVING THE IMPOSSIBLE

Practically Achieving a God-Scripted Life

*The greatest Old or New Testament saints who ever lived
were on a level that is quite within our reach.
The same spiritual power that enabled them to become our
spiritual heroes, is also available to us.*[28]

GOULBURN

five

Leslie

CLEARING THE FOG

removing the clouds that obscure our true purpose

To know Christ is life's greatest achievement.[29]
L. B. COWMAN

It's easy to come up with formulas for following God, complex belief systems that help us clarify why He put us on this earth. But the answer to finding our life's purpose is far simpler than we imagine. In fact, it is so simple that most of us miss it completely in our desperate search for direction.

Clearing the Fog of Complicated Questions

Cara is a fun-loving twenty-eight-year-old who is struggling to find a focus. "I always thought that sometime in my twenties, my life would finally start to make sense," she told us. "But now my twenties are almost over, and I still don't know what to do with my life. I've prayed for answers. But God doesn't seem to be giving me any direction."

Paul is a nineteen-year-old soccer player struggling with decision making. "I'm thinking of going to either a Bible college or a Christian university—how do I know which one God wants for me?" he asked us recently.

Throughout our life, we are faced with these kinds of life-affecting decisions. Should I take the job in Albuquerque or the job in Santa Monica? Should I marry Bob or move to Barcelona? Should I go secular with my singing career or try the Christian route?

So often, we lean on these decisions to define the meaning of our life. We agonize over which college to attend or what ministry to pursue because we believe that those decisions define our life's purpose.

It's easy to come up with formulas for following God, complex belief systems that help us clarify why He put us on this earth. We read books, attend seminars, take personality tests, and try to define our deepest desires—all as part of a crusade to figure out the meaning of our existence.

But the answer to finding our life's purpose is far simpler than we imagine. In fact, it is so simple that most of us miss it completely in our desperate search for direction.

The Secret Revisited

In the previous chapter, we discussed the "secret" that enables us to experience the fullness of a life with God. We found the key to unlock the impossible existence: the exchange of our life for the life of Christ.

Once we make that exchange, it is no longer *us* that work for God; it's now *Christ* working through us. It's no longer us attempting to imitate Him; it's now Christ Himself shining His perfection through our being. It's no longer us miserably failing in our eager expeditions up His Holy Everest; it is now Christ Himself *carrying* us triumphantly up the steep and impossible slopes of His holiness.

And all we must do is *allow* Him to use our body as His holy residence. We must simply *yield* to His Life at work within us. We must simply *let* ourselves be carried in His all-powerful arms up the mountainside in triumph.

That sacred exchange is the secret to the indomitable Christian existence. *And that sacred exchange is the secret to unlocking our life's purpose as well.*

In John 15, Jesus gave His disciples what may be the most profound and beautiful command in the entire Bible. He cleared life of all its complexities and confusion with one simple phrase. He summed up the essence, the grandeur, the mystery, and the marvel of life in but a few life-altering words. He said to them, "Abide in Me."[30]

What did He mean by that?

He meant, "Find the meaning of life *in Me*. Find your value and confidence *in Me*. Find your purpose and direction *in Me*. Find the source for all spiritual achievement *in Me*. Find the strength to live each moment *in Me*. Find the wisdom to navigate the many turns of life *in Me*. Find forgiveness from all your sins *in Me*. Find the satisfaction of boundless joy *in Me*. Find the most glorious peace *in Me*. Find the most perfect love and acceptance *in Me*. Find the most satisfying life for all eternity *in Me*."

To abide in Christ means to allow His Life to possess us at all times and in every situation life brings. To abide means saying to God with the inhaling of every breath, "Not my will, but Yours be done." To abide means sharing in a holy communion with our precious Heavenly Lover, listening to His gentle whisper at every turn of life's drama.

God created us to *abide in Him*. It's that basic. Abiding in Him is our life's purpose. Abiding in Him is what we were created for. Abiding in Him is why we are here.

We are here on this earth to intimately know and enjoy our God. We are here on this earth to let our lives be used, owned, and operated by His almighty grace. We are here to allow His Life to evidence itself through our being. And all these things rolled into one say, we are here on this earth to *abide in Christ*.

Practicing His Presence

Brother Lawrence, a gentle monk who lived in the 1600s, called it "practicing the presence of God." Lawrence made it his utmost endeavor to live with a continual sense of God's presence and to never forget about Him, even for a moment. He worked as a cook in the monastery's kitchen, and as he began his tasks each morning he dedicated his day to his Creator. As he went about his tasks, he conversed in familiar conversation with his Maker, imploring God's grace and offering every action as a sacrifice to Him.[31]

"There is not in the world a kind of life more sweet and delightful than that of a continual conversation with God," wrote Lawrence. "Those only can comprehend it who practice and experience it."[32]

God is far less concerned about what we *do* for Him than He is about our passion to simply *be* with Him. He isn't impressed with numbers or achievements like we are. He is moved by the daily act of surrender. He is stirred by our desire to know Him more.

Choosing the right college, the right career, the right ministry, and the right spouse is important. But most of us become so caught up in trying to make those key decisions that we fail to build on the foundation stone of a successful life—bringing our entire existence under the control of God Almighty every hour of every day. *When we abide in Christ, all the other pieces in our life supernaturally fall into place.*

Two thousand years ago Christ told His first disciples, "First, seek My loving control over your life, My kingdom-rule over your soul, and then I will be sure to take care of all these other details of your life."[33]

Developing a Holy Instinct

As we learn to abide in Christ and practice His presence, something amazing happens within us—something that lifts the confusing fog of decision making and makes our path clear. We develop a holy instinct. Our spiritual ears become tuned to the whisper of God's Spirit. Our spiritual eyes become open to His fingerprints of direction upon our life.

Have you ever heard someone say, "When you meet the love of your life, *you just know*"? Well, that's the way holy instinct works. The more we abide in Christ, the less we have to wonder what specific steps He wants us to take in life. *We will just know.*

In my first decade of marriage to Eric, I have become quite familiar with who he is. Knowing my husband isn't something that just happened naturally; I've made it my priority to study him. I have spent countless hours talking with him, listening to him, and seeking to understand his heart. I have observed him closely. I've watched how he acts when he is hurt, how his face lights up when he is excited, and which words of encouragement give him the strength to keep going. The more I learn to understand his dreams, desires, and feelings, the better I can truly know him.

Because I know Eric so well, I have developed a certain instinct in our marriage. When we have been working on a book project all day and I hear him give a restless sigh around 5 p.m., I instinctively know that he would really love a trip to the local coffee shop for a cup of hot chai (with a squirt of vanilla, his favorite). He doesn't have to say anything, but I am aware of his desire because I know him so well.

Of course, there are times when I ask Eric specific questions, such as "What do you feel like for dinner?" or "How can I be a better wife?" Seeking out his thoughts and desires helps me continue to know Eric better and better each year of our marriage. And he does the same for me.

Gaining a holy instinct toward Christ is similar to cultivating intimacy in marriage. As we spend time in His presence, as we submit to His rule over each area of our life, as we get to know His nature and character, we begin to truly *know Him*. And the more we know Him, the less we have to ask, "Lord, what should I do in this situation?" Because we *know Him,* we instinctively *know* what He would have us do.

As I abide in Christ, I learn to recognize the soft guiding voice of His Spirit within me. I feel Him pointing out people who need my sensitivity. I feel His prick of caution when I begin to head down the wrong path. I feel His sorrow when I make a choice that grieves Him. I know my God, and therefore, I know His voice.

Of course, there are still plenty of times when I ask God specific questions. "Lord, what should I write in this chapter of the book?" or "Lord, should I accept this speaking invitation?" There are times when I feel that He gives me direct answers to these questions. But it is all too easy to get caught up in seeking *answers* rather than in simply seeking *Him*. So when I need to make a decision and no answers seem to be coming my way, I take my focus off of "solving the problem" and simply spend time in the presence of my King. And inevitably, as I focus on Him, the answers become clear.

As I abide in the presence of my King, a holy instinct guides my steps.

Clearing the Fog of Sinful Residue

Samantha is a college sophomore who is hitting some road-blocks in her spiritual life. "I can't seem to hear God's voice," she wrote. "I want to abide in Him, but no matter how much I pray or read my Bible, He just seems distant."

Many of us have felt Samantha's frustration. We long to get closer to God, to know Him so well that a holy instinct rules our life. But we don't know how. Our pursuit of Him seems empty and fruitless. We pray for direction, but He doesn't seem to respond.

Few of us ever realize that to yield to God's Spirit on a moment-to-moment basis often requires some radical life changes. When we have lived a self-ruled existence, we usually have piled up years of sinful residue within our soul. Unconfessed sin, bitterness, jealousy, anger, hatred, and fear are just a few of the roadblocks that clutter up our inner life and hinder our ability to clearly hear the voice of our King. When sinful residue is left unchecked, it entangles our emotions, our thoughts, and our motives. It gives strength to our selfish nature and creates a spiritual fog that quells the holy whisper of God's Spirit.

To build our life around abiding in Christ, we must first remove the fog within our soul so that we can clearly hear His guiding voice. We must thoroughly cleanse our inner life.

Alex is a college student who recently went through an internal cleansing process. Alex asked God to reveal to him any specific things that were hindering his ability to truly abide in Christ. And as he opened himself up to God's Spirit, he soon knew what he had to do.

"As painful as it was," Alex said, "I finally called my parents and repented of the lies I had told them and all the times I had shown them disrespect over the years. I even called friends from my past and asked their forgiveness for being an ungodly example to them."

Alex made some practical changes in his private life as well. "I got rid of all my ungodly music. I threw away magazines and posters that filled my mind with impure thoughts. I even stopped watching TV. Anything that was pulling me away from God, I kicked it out of my life. And the results in my spiritual life have been incredible."

Allowing God's Spirit to lead us through an internal cleansing process has nothing to do with following spiritual "rules" or trying to "appease" Christ by being as perfect as possible; it is something that flows naturally and willingly out of a desire to please our King with every aspect of our existence.

Whenever Eric and I find ourselves struggling to hear God's holy whisper, we are reminded to get on our knees and ask His Spirit to reveal any sin that is lingering in our inner life. When we confess our sin and allow Him to wash us clean, we are able to quickly recognize His voice and bow to His commands.

If you are longing to abide in Christ but find yourself running into roadblocks, consider setting aside a focused period of time for some internal housecleaning. For this process, Eric and I suggest prayerfully working through the section called "Cleansing the Inner Life" on page 203 of this book. This material is very detailed and was designed specifically for the internal cleansing process.

Even if you have walked through a similar "housecleaning" process in the past, it is worthwhile to consider doing it again. The second time around may not be as intense, but it is just as valuable in deepening our intimacy with Christ. Continued cleansing of our inner life is an important part of keeping our spiritual ears tuned to God's voice.

Clearing the Fog of Part-Time Christianity

One Sunday morning, Eric and I were preparing to speak at a church service. It was thirty minutes before the service began, and we were sitting backstage with the worship team. For twenty-nine minutes, the team sipped coffee and chatted about their lives over the past week. They raved about the recently released *Austin Powers* sequel, laughed at the crude jokes they'd heard on *Saturday Night Live,* and bragged about whatever gorgeous guy or girl they happened to be dating that month.

Then thirty seconds before the service started, everyone on the worship team abruptly switched gears. Like Clark Kent morphing into Superman, they suddenly were transformed into completely different people. They instantly cleaned up their language, straightened their posture, and changed their facial expressions from carefree to pious. As they walked onstage and reached for their microphones, they smiled serenely, as if they'd just spent the morning basking in God's glorious presence. They began to utter exclamations of "Praise the Lord!" and "God is good!" as effortlessly as if their every conversation was peppered with such comments. Within the space of one minute, Eric and I had watched these five Christians switch from "real-life mode" into "Christ mode."

Most of us are all too familiar with real-life mode versus Christ mode. For some of us, the switch is less obvious than for the Sunday morning worship team I just described. But still, it is all too easy to split our lives into spiritual and non-spiritual categories. During our daily life, as we interact with friends and watch movies and pursue our dreams, we rarely pause to listen to the soft inner voice of God's Spirit.

But when we walk into a church building or a gathering of Christians, we switch into Christ mode. We close our eyes, lift our hands, and sway to worship songs about His glory. We bow our heads and nod in agreement as prayers of commitment to Him are prayed. But the minute we walk out the door, we are once again consumed with worry, fear, discouragement, bitterness, or personal ambition. We quickly switch out of Christ mode and go back to living self-ruled and self-constructed lives.

The reason that so many of us struggle with abiding in Christ is because we are clouded by the fog of *part-time Christianity*.

To truly abide in Christ, we must determine that every day, every hour, and every minute will revolve around *Him*, not us. We must become like eager servants, standing by the chair of our Master, awaiting His next request, willing to do whatever it takes to please Him.

Brother Lawrence learned to practice God's presence by

living as if he and God were the only ones in the world. "Every day, every hour, every minute, even in the height of my business—I drove away from my mind everything that was capable of interrupting my thought of God," he wrote.[34]

It is only when we drown out all other voices and become a servant who bows to His commands that we can experience the mystery of abiding in Christ—allowing Him to live *His* Life through our body, transforming us into *His* image from the inside out.

Learning to abide in Christ involves a lifetime of building deeper intimacy with Him, constantly discovering new aspects of His love and grace. And it is important to realize that He does not demand that we become the "finished prod-uct" overnight. This side of heaven, we may never reach the highest pinnacle of Mount Everest Christianity, where we abide in Him every second of every moment of every hour of every day. But what matters is that we aim our life in that direction, starting today.

Putting It into Action

If you are struggling to abide in Christ throughout the day, it's important to evaluate the practical side of your life. Are you building your life around Him, not just in theory, but in reality? Your personal hindrance to a Christ-built life may be something as simple as the time you spend in front of the computer every day. Allow God to show you anything in your life that needs to be restructured in order to make knowing Him your true priority. Get some focused time alone with God and allow His Spirit to show you the answers to the fol-lowing questions:

1. Are there activities or relationships in my life that pull me away from God? What steps must I take to remove those things from my life?
2. Are there ungodly influences that distract me from my true purpose? What steps must I take to remove those things from my life?
3. What practical changes in my life must be made for me to build my life around Christ? For example, do I need to get up earlier? Cut out some activities? Pull away from certain friendships? Watch fewer movies? Spend less time on the computer? Watch less TV? Eliminate one or more of these things completely?

When we evaluate our lives, too often we ask the wrong questions. "There's nothing wrong with having friends, is there?" we sputter irritably, unwilling to give up a thriving social life. "What's wrong with a little relaxation in front of the TV?" we spout defensively, unwilling to sacrifice our *Seinfeld* reruns. "God doesn't expect me to go live in a cave somewhere, does He?" we mumble sarcastically, unwilling to appear strange to the world around us.

When God asks us to say good-bye to the things we cling to most tightly, it doesn't necessarily mean those things are wrong in and of themselves. But often, those things have such a hold over us that they stand in the way of our ability to truly abide in Christ.

As modern Christians, we are constantly trying to serve ourselves and God at the same time. We try to perform the ultimate balancing act, feeding our own selfish whims while staying on God's "good side" by living as morally as possible.

But the true Christian life is not a balancing act. It is a *daily act of total surrender*. Let God's Spirit reveal what practical changes you need to make in order to structure your life around your true purpose—abiding in Him. And whatever He asks you to do, don't hesitate another moment before obeying.

A life that abides in Christ is the only life worth living.

❧

I am the vine, you are the branches;
he who abides in Me and I in him,
he bears much fruit,
for apart from Me you can do nothing.[35]

JESUS CHRIST

In a Nutshell

We try to complicate life, but life is really all about one thing: abiding in Christ each and every day. It's not about choosing the right college, the right spouse, the right career, or the right name for our first kid. Sure, God cares about the small details of our lives, but until we get the right foundation in place, the small details have nothing upon which to build.

A well-lived life isn't one that seeks after money, prestige, or position; it's one that seeks after more and more of Jesus Christ. As we intimately familiarize ourselves with our King, we gain a holy sense of His desires. And as our intimate communion with Him grows, we instinctively begin to know how to live our lives for Him and what He would have us do in every small decision-making moment of life. As we move ourselves out of the way more and more and allow Christ full and complete access to our existence, the power of Christ alive inside us explodes like a brilliant fireworks display in our lives.

six

Eric

ADVENTURE TRAINING

calibrating our minds for the challenge of frontier life

> *All my devotion is an insult to God unless*
> *every bit of my practical life squares*
> *with Jesus Christ's demands.*[36]
>
> OSWALD CHAMBERS

We believe that as long as we are doing the basics—attending church, reading our Bible, maybe going on a mission trip once in a while—then we are flexing our spiritual muscles. But most of us have barely scratched the surface of our potential for spiritual strength.

God's Adventure Training School

As the story goes, a traveling evangelist in England back in the eighteenth century was asked to appear before one of the most prestigious and influential men in the country. Many had sought an audience with this rich lord, but only a few were granted the illustrious privilege of his company for an evening.

The evangelist welcomed the opportunity to share a meal with this man, who was interested in understanding more about the evangelist's work for Christ throughout the English countryside. But as night waxed on and the clock struck seven, the evangelist rose from the table and declared plainly, "Thank you for a wonderful evening, but I must be going."

Startled by the man's impertinence and disregard for English custom, the rich lord replied, "Do you not know that my table is the most highly sought after table in England? I receive hundreds of requests each day to gain my audience, and you have the audacity to remove yourself before our night is through?"

The humble evangelist looked back with a startling confidence in his eyes and said, "I have an appointment with the Lord of heaven and earth, and I dare not be tired and I dare not be late."

Martin Luther, the mighty Christian reformer, spent the best three hours of his day with God, even if it meant rising at four in the morning. John Wesley, the heroic eighteenth-century evangelist, spent at least two hours a day in prayer, no matter how many other tasks called for his attention. Edward Payson, a true inspiration to the church in his time, was known to have worn grooves into the floorboards where his knees pressed so often and so long during prayer.[37]

Great heroes of the faith accomplished incredible things in their lifetimes. They wrote hundreds of books, preached thousands of sermons, and reformed entire societies. Their amazing spiritual vitality did not come from a few minutes of hurried prayer each morning or attending church every Sunday. Rather, they built their *entire lives* around a relationship with Christ. They gave their best hours of the day to God. They walked away from once-in-a-lifetime opportunities simply to be with their King. Some even wore out their floorboards from kneeling in prayer. Inconceivable? Preposterous? Quite the contrary. This is historical reality.

How many of us today possess that kind of spiritual discipline? How many of us have that kind of unswerving, unfaltering commitment to God? How many of us are so devoted to Him that we count time spent in His presence more valuable than any other opportunity that comes our way? If knowing God is our true purpose, then we must make our relationship with Him our highest priority. Not just in theory, but in every moment of the day.

We tend to believe that as long as we are doing the basics—attending church, reading our Bible, maybe going on a mission trip once in a while—then we are flexing our spiritual muscles. But most of us have barely scratched the surface of our potential for spiritual strength.

To become the real-life action heroes God calls us to be, we must enroll in His adventure training school. It's a training program more intense than any Olympic practice schedule. It requires everything we are, every moment of the day. It calls for 100 percent devotion. Halfhearted or part-time participants need not apply.

A mountain climber spends years rigorously training several hours a day to prepare for a trek up Everest. To experience the lifetime of spiritual adventure that awaits us, we too must devote ourselves—heart, soul, mind, and strength—to the training and discipline of our spiritual life.

In God's training school, we will learn to practically restructure our lives around our true purpose, abiding in Christ. To abide in Christ is to become more and more like Him in every area of life. To abide in Christ is to practice His presence each moment of the day. And to abide in Christ like that does not come without a serious regimen of training. We're talking about a lifetime of focus, dedication, and commitment.

It is important to understand that if we try to develop spiritual discipline for the wrong reasons, the attempt will be futile and the results empty. Some of us seek a spiritually disciplined life in order to "appease" God, thinking we can personally atone for our failures through hard work and effort. But this approach will only lead to a legalistic, imprisoned life.

Genuine spiritual growth happens only when we are fully yielded to the Spirit of Christ and motivated by a passionate desire to know our King. But we must rely on the *supernatural* power of *Christ in us* to achieve this.

Mysterious or Mechanical?

An energetic young man named Micah approached me last week with an interesting question. "What part do I play in my spiritual growth?" he wanted to know. "How much of it just happens supernaturally, and how much should I do myself?"

Micah's question is one that many of us wonder. How do we practically strengthen our spiritual life, yet lean completely on the power of Christ in us?

Oswald Chambers calls this the balance between the mysterious and the mechanical. "We have to recognize that we are one half mechanical and one half mysterious," says Chambers. "To live in either domain and ignore the other is to be a fool or a fanatic. To believe in the mysterious work of God's grace but then ignore the fact that we have to work it out in our mechanical life produces spiritual humbugs; those who make a divorce between the mysterious life and the practical life."[38]

In other words, we must *practically* (or mechanically) structure every aspect of our life to facilitate the *supernatural* (or mysterious) work of God's Spirit within us. It isn't enough to merely acknowledge what Christ has done for us; we must allow that glorious reality to permeate every part of our practical existence.

James 4:8 says "Draw near to God and He will draw near to you."[39] Those simple words contain the answer to Micah's question. When we seek Him with all our heart, He allows us to find Him. When we pursue Him with every fiber of our being, He draws closer to us than we could ever imagine. The Spirit of Christ working in and through us is truly a supernatural phenomenon. But to fully experience that mystery, we must structure our life around knowing Him, abiding in Him, and pursuing more of Him. When we draw near to Christ, He draws near to us.

All too many of us put minimal effort into our relationship with Christ and yet expect maximum results. We long for John Wesley's unshakable boldness. We wish we had Oswald Chamber's profound grasp of Truth. We envy D. L. Moody's contagious spiritual passion. But we fail to realize that every great man or woman of God who made a truly eternal impact upon this world didn't just play at Christianity—they devoted their every waking breath to the pursuit of Jesus Christ.

They spent their best hours each day alone in God's presence, in heartfelt communion with their King. They arose before the sun was up, awakening the dawn with their songs of worship. They spent their life digging deeply into God's Word, poring over the Scriptures for hours at a time. They sacrificed comforts, popularity, financial stability, and the respect of others in order to build their lives around Christ.

God's real-life action heroes enter His adventure training school and never look back. They train every part of their being—mind, body, and soul—to facilitate the supernatural work of God's Spirit within them. And the result is a vibrant, victorious, world-changing life that Hollywood cannot hope to imitate.

If you are ready for that kind of life, prepare to embark on a lifelong journey of devotion and discipline. The journey is rigorous, grueling, intense, and painful. But is it the most fulfilling, exhilarating life we could ever hope for.

God's adventure training school involves two important disciplines:

1. Training the mind.
2. Training the body.

The rest of this chapter is devoted to the first of these two areas, training our minds for Christlike navigation of the frontier life. In the next chapter, we will explore disciplining our bodies for heroic spiritual action.

So grab your training shoes and fill up your supersized water bottle.

You're about to enter spiritual boot camp.

Training the Mind

Once I read a pamphlet that said Jesus Christ was returning for His children on one of four dates in September of 1988.

The author of this pamphlet even gave eighty-eight reasons why this was a Biblical fact and not just a theory.

Like a gullible walleye, I bought it hook, line, and sinker.

I was a senior in high school at the time. My English teacher had assigned a term paper, but I knew that by the time it was due I would be long gone thanks to September's Rapture. I remember watching my classmates furiously compile their research and thinking, *Poor, poor people. While you are stressing about your term papers, I will be skipping through heavenly meadows.*

I didn't research my topic. I didn't begin writing my paper. In fact, I ignored all of my school assignments that month. After all, why should I put any effort into schoolwork if I wasn't even going to be around to receive my grade? I had better things to do during my last month on earth. I didn't want to waste these days writing term papers, tackling trigonometric riddles, and dissecting frogs.

The prophesied dates came and went. With a sinking heart, I realized that the opportune days for Christ's return had passed without incident, which was more than I could say for my grades. It took about two weeks of begging for extra credit assignments before I was finally able to salvage my self-sabotaged report card.

But I found I had gained a new philosophy on life: Live each day as if it were my last, but expect to be here for a lifetime.

Unfortunately, that story is just a taste of my early Christian delusions. I had many other experiences that were laced with ignorance and coated with humiliation. I went through a phase of praying the same words over and over again, thinking that God responded to repetition. There was a season when I thought that going to a "revival meeting" was the only way to experience revival. I remember believing that if my hands tingled during a prayer service, it meant I had received the gift of healing. At one time, I thought that raising my arms really high while singing would cause God to hear my voice above all the others. Oh, and I used to think that if I didn't say, "in the name of Jesus Christ, amen," at the end of my prayer, then the whole prayer didn't count and I had to start over.

I was sincere, but my sincerity didn't save me from being wrong. And the reason I was wrong was because I didn't really *know* my God. I never took the time to acquaint myself with His nature and align myself with His Truth. Instead, I borrowed the thoughts and ideas of others and adopted them as my own. But I was borrowing from others who probably borrowed *their* ideas from others. If I had really been in touch with my God, I would have instinctively known how *unlike* God some of my perceptions were.

Too many of us blindly follow the prescriptions of other well-meaning Christians, only to find ourselves heading *away* from Christ as a result. One of the best ways to protect the life of Christ within us is to sharpen our minds and focus our thoughts around His Truth. When we learn to think and reason biblically, we can be confident in what we believe and why. And then we are far less likely to be misled by others.

The True Test

The book of Acts describes a group of Berean synagogue leaders who listened with great eagerness to the gospel message brought by Paul and Silas. The Bible says these men were "noble-minded…examining the Scriptures daily to see whether these things were so."[40] When it comes to evaluating the books we read, the songs we sing, and the messages we hear, it is all too easy to accept what we are told based on how it makes us *feel,* rather than on how it lines up with the unchanging Word of God. But to train our minds to think like Christ, we must become like the Bereans, making the Bible our foundation from which to reason.

Sadly, many subtle lies have crept into modern Christian teaching, and all too many of us are completely oblivious to the danger. One of the primary reasons we blindly accept false teaching is that we rarely devote much time or energy to studying the Word of God. As a result, our spiritual senses become dull, making us susceptible to deception. We use our emotions to guide us rather than God's unchanging Truth, and therefore, our steps become faulty and unstable.

Danny is a young Christian who heard a message at church one Sunday morning that changed his life. The guest speaker that day gave a passionate speech, exhorting his audience to claim their God-given right to wealth and happiness. Danny was deeply moved by the man's convincing words, and from that day on, he oriented his life around the pursuit of money. Of course, he cloaks his desire for riches in lofty, spiritual-sounding ideals. "Once I am wealthy, then I can really help the poor," he reasons.

Danny fails to see that the path he's chosen does not line up with a key scriptural truth: "You cannot serve God and wealth."[41]

Hayley, an outgoing college senior, recently heard a message on evangelism that inspired her. "In order to reach society with the gospel message," said the speaker, "we must become more like the world around us." The speaker encouraged believers to witness to nonbelievers by participating in worldly activities along with them. And so Hayley has begun rejecting her "sheltered" Christian background. She's started drinking, attending wild parties, telling perverted jokes, and listening to raunchy music with her non-Christian friends. "People need to realize that Christianity doesn't produce a bunch of uptight Goody Two-shoes," Hayley says. "I need to show my friends that even though I'm a Christian, I'm also just a real person who likes to have fun."

Hayley fails to understand that the path she's chosen contradicts a foundational scriptural principle: "Do not be conformed to this world."[42]

Unfortunately, these are just a few of the many pitfalls of modern Christian teaching. It is so important that we learn to be watchful, evaluating and testing every message we hear and philosophy we encounter against the infallible Word of God. Only when we take time to delve deep into God's Word and fill our minds with Truth can we avoid the many traps the enemy has laid for us. When we gain a clear understanding of biblical principles, we sharpen our spiritual awareness and lay the foundation for success in every area of life.

Putting It into Action

When it comes to Bible study, few of us even know where to begin.

Chris, a twenty-year-old swing-dancing enthusiast, says that even the thought of studying his Bible is overwhelming. "The only way I ever study my Bible is to flop it open randomly and start reading," he told me. "And half the time it doesn't make any sense to me."

Megan, a young business-school student, understands this frustration. "I know I should be studying the Bible, but I find myself gravitating toward other books instead," she wrote. "It's not that I don't want to understand Scripture; it's just that I have no idea where to start."

Studying the Bible does not have to be a tedious, daunting ordeal. In fact, it can be one of the most exciting, life-giving activities we participate in. It just takes a little planning and a lot of commitment. There are many different methods and theories about how to study the Bible, but here are a few basics that can help get you going. These are the things that Leslie and I have found most helpful in our own study of God's Word.

1. Set Specific Goals

Leslie and I have found that it works well to spend a period of time—several days or weeks—studying one specific book of the Bible. We often study a book of the Bible for an entire month. If there is a certain book or section of the Bible you feel drawn to, then plan to devote a specific period of time to the study of that text. If you aren't sure where to start, we suggest a medium-length book from the New Testament, such as Ephesians, Philippians, or Colossians. But the important thing is to set a goal and stick with it. Once you have a clear picture of where you are headed, it will be far easier to devote focused time to biblical study.

2. Learn Inductive Bible Study

To develop your study skills further, consider joining an inductive Bible study program, either individually or with a group. Inductive Bible study is the process of shaping your thoughts and ideas around Scriptural truths, rather than trying to shape Scriptural truths around your own thoughts and ideas. Most of us are prone to interpret Scripture through our own subjective point of view, rather than allowing Scripture to speak for itself and change our way of thinking. Many churches offer inductive Bible studies. And even if you can't find one in your area, you can learn inductive Bible study on your own. One of our favorite resources for inductive Bible study is Precept Ministries International, which can be found on-line at www.precept.org. Another great resource to help you get started is Howard Hendricks's book *Living by the Book* (Moody).

3. Look for Practical Application

Instead of just reading the words of Scripture, it is vitally important that we personally apply the principles of Scripture to our lives. As you study the Bible, prayerfully consider how you can apply what you are reading in your everyday life. Leslie and I find it helpful to ask ourselves the question, *What does this Scripture mean for me personally?* We find it beneficial to put our answers in writing. This helps us to fully express our thoughts, as well as hold ourselves accountable to making practical changes in our life as a result of what we have read in God's Word.

Studying God's Word is an incredible experience, one that will give you solid footing from which to build a successful Christian life. Don't put it off. Once you develop a focused biblical study plan and begin to see the words of Scripture come alive, you'll wonder why you waited so long to begin.

*The mark of a life governed by the Holy Spirit
is that such a life is continually and ever
more and more occupied with Christ,
that Christ becomes greater and greater as time goes on.*[43]

T. AUSTIN-SPARKS

In a Nutshell

The endless frontier that God has called us to explore is not an easy journey. It's a challenging expedition, full of steep mountain passes and dangerous white-water crossings. And along the way, we will face countless allurements and justifications that try to pull us in the wrong direction. The voice of compromise constantly whispers in our ear, *Follow me. I know an easier, safer, more comfortable way.* But if we give in to compromise, we will soon find ourselves headed away from God's holy mountain and straight into the valley of defeat.

That is why God wants to train His adventurers to think as He thinks. He desires to equip His action heroes with an intimate acquaintance of Him, so that any and all counterfeits are instantly recognized and avoided. To do this, we must study our God's heart, understand His unchanging Truth, and search out His ways. We must explore His holy Scriptures, which enunciate His thoughts, His ideas, His plans, and His design for each of our lives.

When God's thoughts overtake the human mind, they expose all that is contrary to Him. When our minds are grounded in God's Truth, we gain the strength to remain on His straight and narrow road—the only road that leads to a victorious life in Him.

seven

Eric

FRONTIER ENDURANCE

training our bodies for the heroic expedition ahead

> *When the heart sees what God wants,*
> *the body must be willing to spend*
> *and be spent for that cause alone.*[44]
> OSWALD CHAMBERS

Most of us believe that doing what we want, when we want is our natural right. But in God's adventure training school, we learn to ignore the all-consuming demands of our selfish bodies. Our physical desires no longer rule; they must yield to the Spirit of Christ within.

The Tomato Soup Story

A dozen or so years ago, my biggest struggle in life was my stomach. No, it didn't bulge out from under my shirt. The problem was, it was always growling for more food. Unfortunately, I was a missionary at the time, living on diddly-squat missionary rations.

When I was growing up, my mom always fixed enough food every night to feed a small country. And during my years of college dorm life, every night was an all-you-can-eat buffet. I would usually have four empty plates on my tray by the time dinner was over. Sometimes I even went out and grabbed the "five burgers for two bucks" deal at Zip's Hamburger Stand afterwards to top it all off.

So to put it mildly, I wasn't at all prepared for the measly portions of food that missionaries have to deal with. My stomach hadn't stopped growling since I said, "Yes, Lord, I'll go!"

I was in Michigan, working as a missionary alongside my sister, and our food budget was pretty sparse. I still ate better than most people in this world, but it was nothing compared to my upbringing, and I complained constantly. It was right about this time that I read the scripture, their "god is their appetite."[45] Whoa, was that convicting! That verse was talking about *me*. My life had revolved around my stomach ever since I was two and encountered my very first M&M.

Now I realized that something had to be done to show God that He wasn't second fiddle to my beloved fried chicken and cheesecake. So to solve my stomach problem, I decided I would fast for seven days. Though I had fasted for short periods of time before, a week without food was new territory for me. But this was important. I had to somehow prove that my god wasn't really my appetite.

That week was one of the most miserable experiences of my entire life. I thought about food the entire time. I knew I was supposed to be praying and doing all sorts of spiritual things throughout the week, but my mind kept gravitating toward food. Every night I dreamed of pasta primavera, and every morning I awoke with an insatiable craving for roast beef.

I'll never forget the final day of my self-imposed fast. I figured that, technically, I could end my fast at the stroke of midnight and still have it count as a weeklong fast. I read through nearly every one of my sister's cookbooks that day, dreaming about what I would eat when the clock struck twelve.

Now experts recommend that to end a long fast, you should eat soup rather than heavy stuff like meat or pasta. I longed for a steak, but by now even watery broth sounded heavenly, so I spent the entire four hours leading up to midnight preparing a huge pot of tomato soup. It smelled so good! I kept my nose over the pot for nearly an hour while stirring in basil leaves, dumping in plenty of salt and pepper, and imagining how it was going to taste.

At midnight I had my tomato soup already in the bowl and my spoon already in hand. I devoured that soup like a desert wanderer slurps at the waters of an oasis. I couldn't get enough. I ate bowl after bowl after bowl of the creamy red stuff.

When I finally came up for air, I was as sick as a dog. I had deprived my poor stomach for seven days and then consumed a month's supply of tomatoes in the space of three and a half minutes. I spent the rest of the night in misery, groaning from the pain and wondering why I had ever even *looked* at a tomato.

To this day, my stomach turns when someone offers me tomato soup.

﹏

When we attempt to train our physical life prior to giving God control over our body, our efforts can quickly turn into a comedic display of wimpy human willpower. *Self-imposed* discipline looks similar on the outside to *God-directed* discipline, but it produces a completely different result; it's empty human effort as opposed to God at work within us. And for all our sweat and tears, it doesn't even work. Self-imposed discipline fails every time—it discourages us and gives even more power to the weakness we are trying to whip.

But *Christ-initiated, Christ-enabled* physical discipline will make our spiritual life thrive. Paul the apostle said, "I discipline my body and make it my slave, so that, after I have preached to others, I myself will not be disqualified."[46] Our decision to pursue a God-scripted adventure will be fruitless if it is only a spiritual and mental commitment; it must be a physical one as well. When we allow our physical desires to control us, we cannot be controlled by the Spirit of Christ within us.

Our culture is extremely used to creature comforts. We have the ability to satisfy virtually every craving with the snap of our fingers. If we feel like eating a greasy hamburger, we merely have to swing by the local drive-through. If we are longing for chocolate cheesecake, we can stop at a nearby café. If we want to be entertained by world-class actors and multimillion-dollar special effects, we only have to tune in our satellite dish or whip out our Blockbuster card. And if we desire to sleep the day away in a soft, comfortable bed, we simply have to switch off our alarm clock and pull the covers over our head.

There's nothing intrinsically wrong with comforts like these. And yet we can easily become so accustomed to them that they rule our life. Most of us have become so spoiled and comfortable that we lack the physical discipline to build our life around what truly matters—pursuing more of Christ each day. It's all too easy to justify sleeping for an extra half hour and missing our quiet time, or relaxing in front of a movie on DVD instead of nurturing our relationship with Christ.

Most of us believe that doing *what* we want, *when* we want is our natural right. We balk at the thought of "disciplining our body and making it our slave" in order to stay spiritually sharp and strong. But in God's adventure training school, that's exactly what it takes. We have to start ignoring the all-consuming demands of our selfish bodies. Our physical desires must no longer rule; they must yield to the Spirit of Christ within.

Identifying Areas of Weakness

We all have different areas of physical weakness. I'm not talking about the inability to twist open the super-tight lid on a jar of pickles or getting winded after running up the stairs. What I mean is our tendency to give in to certain physical cravings at the expense of our relationship with Christ. It might be a habit of oversleeping that results in minimal time spent alone with our King. It could be an addiction to movies, television, or the Internet that stymies our spiritual growth. Or maybe it is a love of eating that causes us to turn to food for comfort and happiness, rather than to our Lord.

I used to be addicted to exercise. If I ever missed a workout, I would become edgy and irritable. I was controlled by the need to look toned and fit, and time at the gym had become a higher priority than time with God. So for a season of my life, I stopped working out completely. I felt that God wanted me to break my addiction to physical fitness and simply learn to be still and content in His presence. Once I rebuilt my life and priorities around Christ and relinquished my desire to look a certain way, physical fitness became a balanced, healthy part of my lifestyle. It no longer controlled me or trumped my relationship with God.

Ask God's Spirit to reveal what *your* particular weaknesses are. And then prayerfully consider what steps you can take to overcome those controlling habits. Do you need to start forcing yourself out of bed an hour earlier each morning for a time of prayer and Bible study? Or how about turning off your TV and reading Christian biographies at night?

A young man named Jeremy recently told me that he had begun sleeping on the floor every night in order to train his body for life on the mission field. And a girl named Natalie shared that she has found fasting regularly to be a wonderful blend of physical and spiritual discipline. (And just for the record, she doesn't end her fasts with five bowls of tomato soup.) Whatever steps you feel God asking you to take in order to train your body to yield to His control, don't hesitate to obey. Training in this area may be painful and uncomfortable at first, but the rewards in your relationship with Christ will be incredible.

Remember, physical discipline should never flow from a desire to "appease" God or atone for our shortcomings by punishing our bodies. Our commitment to train the body should flow from a longing to build every aspect of our being around the pursuit of Jesus Christ. Just as great athletes train morning and night, through rain or shine, simply to excel at the sports they love, so we must train to grow ever closer to the God we love. And we must rely on the power of Christ in us for the strength to succeed.

If you find that physical discipline is an especially difficult challenge, consider recruiting a godly teammate to help keep you on the right track. Share your specific commitments with your teammate and invite this person to hold you accountable to those goals. If possible, meet regularly to pray together and share your struggles and victories. Involving another person can provide a tremendous boost toward breaking our unhealthy habits and retraining ourselves to yield to God's Spirit rather than our fleshly wants.

The Physical Discipline of Prayer

Prayer is not only a physical discipline; it's a spiritual one as well. But if we never discipline our physical life around time with God, our prayer life can never begin to flourish in the spiritual realm.

David awoke the dawn with his passionate prayers.[47] Most of us can hardly stay awake through a five-minute prayer time, let alone awaken the dawn with heartfelt prayers that shake the heavens. We often think of praying as a tedious obligation, a few textbook phrases that we utter each day in order to feel more spiritual. But true prayer is so much more than throwing some rushed requests in God's direction, hoping that He happens to be listening. True prayer is a passionate encounter with the King of all kings. True prayer is the music of heaven, a beautiful symphony of adoration and supplication in the throne room of almighty God. If you don't believe me, just read through the Psalms.

To graduate from mediocre mutterings to prayers that shake the heavens, we must devote ourselves to developing the discipline of prayer. There is no formula for proper prayer, but there are things we can do to cultivate a more effective prayer life.

Building Our Schedule Around Prayer

Amy Carmichael, a lifelong missionary to India, once wrote that if we want to awake the dawn with our prayers, we must avoid being entangled by the countless social distractions that pull us in every direction.[48] Leslie and I have found this to be very true. We have learned to choose our friendships, social activities, and outside commitments very carefully. It is all too easy to cram our schedule with busyness—even if we are busy doing "good" things—to the point that we have little energy left over for effective prayer times. We try not to let anything, no matter how important it seems, interfere with our prayer life. This often means making social and career sacrifices, but the rewards are more than worth it.

Leslie and I find that the best time for uninterrupted quiet is early in the morning. When we get up early and devote our first hours of the day to time with God, we are less likely to be distracted by a ringing phone or doorbell. And prayer in the morning gives us the right foundation for the rest of the day. But to be able to wake up early to meet with God, we have to be disciplined about getting to bed at a decent hour. So we often say no to activities that will keep us up late. And if we ever have to make an exception, we restructure our schedule the following morning to allow for adequate prayer time, even if it means we don't accomplish much else that day.

Whether you build your prayer times into the early morning hours or find that another time of day works best, the important thing is to carefully guard your prayer sessions as a precious treasure. Balance your activities and commitments so that you remain alert and fresh for your times with God. And take whatever measures are necessary to remove all distractions, whether that means unplugging the phone or turning off the computer.

When you build your schedule around regular meetings with your Lord, the benefits to your spiritual life will be beyond compare.

The Power of a Prayer Journal

In college, I was deeply impacted by the book *No Compromise*. It's about the spiritual journey of a young musician named Keith Green. Green documented his relationship with Christ by keeping journals in which he put his prayers on paper and recorded his struggles and victories. I began my own journal that year, and I have kept one ever since. I've found journaling to be amazingly profitable to my prayer life. Writing my prayers helps me solidify my thoughts and keeps my mind from wandering. And being able to read back through my old journals and see how God worked in my life strengthens and deepens my faith.

If your prayer life needs a boost, consider starting a prayer journal. Journaling doesn't have to be a complicated process. Simply pour out your heart to God on paper. Periodically look back over your journal entries, and you will be stunned at how much God has done in your life. For some inspiration in this area, I recommend you read books about great Christians who kept prayer journals, such as *No Compromise* or *Shadow of the Almighty: The Life and Testament of Jim Elliot*.

The subject of prayer deserves an entire book, and there are many wonderful books on prayer written by great Christians. My personal favorite is the classic *Power Through Prayer* by E. M. Bounds.

It's important to realize that prayer is something we can learn and grow in for the rest of our lives. It takes time and focus to develop a flourishing prayer life. And even if yours doesn't thrive right away, don't get discouraged. As you draw near to God by entering His throne room with heartfelt prayer, He will draw nearer and nearer to you.

The Physical Discipline of Stillness

Hudson Taylor, a pioneer of missions work in China, eloquently described the antidote for stress. "Are you in a hurry, flurried, distressed?" he wrote, "Look up! Let the face of Jesus shine upon you—the face of the Lord Jesus Christ. Is He worried, troubled, distressed? There is no wrinkle on His brow, no least shade of anxiety. Yet the [problems you face] are His as much as yours."[49]

Hudson Taylor did not have an easy life. He frequently faced poverty, hunger, death threats, and the tragic loss of loved ones. And yet he discovered the secret to overcoming anxiety and stress: "Casting all your anxiety on Him, because He cares for you."[50]

When we look at life from our limited human perspective, it seems there is always plenty to worry and stress about. What we need is to look at our circumstances from a heavenly perspective. When we remain still in God's presence, we soon realize there is nothing to fear. Our God is not shaken by any circumstance. And when we slow down enough to finally see things through His eyes, we will experience "peace...which surpasses all comprehension."[51]

Stillness takes practice. We are habitually consumed with problems, fears, and worries. And often we don't let go of those distractions even during our times alone with God. It's easy to pray about a problem but not really *give* the problem to God. We may ask God to help us with a challenge, but often we continue to stress about it and try to solve it in our own strength. But to cast our cares upon God means to lay them at His feet and leave them there.

Next time you feel the cares of life weighing you down, steal away to a quiet place and practice stillness in God's presence. Ignore your body's apathy and your mind's distraction. Train yourself to be still before God. Place your worries at His feet. Allow Him to do whatever He wants in the situation you are facing, even if it is not the outcome you were hoping for. His ways are perfect, and though we can't always see it at first, His faithfulness is beyond our understanding. He cares more about our life than even we do, and He only wants the best for us. Take some time to read His Word and be reminded that He sees everything and worries about nothing. The more you put this physical discipline of stillness into practice, the more it will become a way of life.

Putting It into Action

God's adventure training school will take us far beyond the mental and physical disciplines discussed in these couple of chapters. What we have discussed here is merely a starting point. It's important to remember that strengthening our spiritual muscles is a lifelong journey of discovery and growth. In focusing on spiritual discipline, our goal is not to become an instant "spiritual giant," but rather to take the first steps toward practically building our life around abiding in Christ. If we will offer our bodies as a living sacrifice to Him, He will take care of the rest.

To make God's adventure training even more applicable to your own personal walk, we encourage you to prayerfully work through the material in Part III of this book, *Frontier Field Guide: A Study Guide for Shaping the Inner Life,* starting on page 139. This material is detailed and extremely practical. It is designed to help you explore God's unique plan for *your* life and deepen your relationship with Him. Our hope is that it will serve as a catalyst to help you experience the boundless depths of your own God-scripted adventure.

> *May we never run from the difficult lesson*
> *or flinch from the rod of discipline.*
> *Richer will be our crown, and sweeter will Heaven be,*
> *if we cheerfully endure to the end.*
> *Then we will graduate in glory.*[52]
> THEODORE L. CUYLER

In a Nutshell

Heroic Christians are those who don't just believe the right things, but do the right things as a result of their beliefs. They are never satisfied with where they are today in their spiritual growth; they are always eager to grow more. But spiritual growth doesn't happen without physical discipline. For our spiritual life to flourish, we must train our bodies to yield not to our own selfish whims, but to the commands of God's Spirit. We must train our physical life to serve our highest priority—abiding in the King of all kings.

Some of us spend hours a day training to be great at a sport or musical talent, but few of us devote hours each day to training for spiritual excellence. God's real-life action heroes aren't shaped through comfort and coddling. The super-conquerors in Christ's kingdom are those willing to come under the rigorous discipline of God's adventure training school.

eight

Leslie

THE ART OF MAPMAKING

boldly leading others into the endless frontier

> *Give me one hundred preachers who fear nothing but sin*
> *and desire nothing but God, and I care not a straw whether*
> *they be clergymen or laymen; such alone will shake the*
> *gates of hell and set up the kingdom of heaven on earth.*[53]
>
> JOHN WESLEY

The Christ-built life is the most thrilling and satisfying existence of all. It is also the most dangerous journey we will ever embark upon. And before our life can become a map for others to follow, we must first count the cost.

Encounters with Real-Life Action Heroes

His name was Polycarp. And he lived a life that counted.

He was a first- and second-century bishop at Smyrna who was condemned to be burned alive for his faith in Christ. Many Christians had already been violently killed for their faith in Christ, and some were caving under the torture, denying Christ and swearing allegiance to Caesar. But not Polycarp.

As the flames leapt around him, Polycarp looked up to heaven, praising God and thanking Him that he was counted worthy to take the cup of Christ. Polycarp's death did not strike terror in the onlooking Christians, as was Caesar's intent. Rather, the believers saw his unshakable courage and joy in the face of death and became even more resolved to stand firm in their faith.[54]

Polycarp's life became a map that would lead others into the endless frontier of a Christ-built life. He bravely pioneered uncharted territory and beckoned his fellow explorers to follow in his footsteps. And when they saw the powerful trail he had blazed for them, they too gained the strength to face even death for their true King.

His name was William Tyndale. And he lived a life that counted.

Tyndale was a theologian and scholar in England in the early sixteenth century, during a time of widespread church corruption. Church leaders interpreted the Scriptures for the common people, who had no Bible in their own language. Those who defied the church or its teachings were burned at the stake.

Despite the danger, Tyndale made it his life's work to develop an accurate English translation of the Bible that could be read by every person who desired it. Tyndale's Bibles were outlawed, seized, and burned. Eventually, he was thrown into prison and killed by the authorities. But his death was not in vain. In fact, his very last words were, "Lord, open the king of England's eyes!" And God answered that prayer. Not long after Tyndale's death, the king ordered that a copy of his translated Bible be placed in every church in England, exhorting the common people to read it. Tyndale's Bible paved the way for the Reformation in England and served as the foundation for the King James Version a century later.[55]

Tyndale's life became a map that would lead others into the endless frontier of a Christ-built life. He bravely pioneered uncharted territory and beckoned his fellow explorers to follow in his footsteps. And when they saw the powerful trail he had blazed for them, they too gained the courage to give their very lives for the preservation of the true gospel of Christ.

Her name was Gladys Aylward. And she lived a life that counted.

Aylward was a household servant in England early in the twentieth century who gave her life to Christ at the age of twenty-six. Without funds or support, she traveled alone to China during a time when believers were facing death and violence at the hands of communists and Japanese invaders. Leaning on the grace and power of God, Aylward rescued children from slavery, shared the gospel with hundreds, and even single-handedly stopped a bloody riot at a men's prison. When her city fell under attack, she escorted nearly one hundred orphan children on foot through enemy territory—a five-and-a-half week journey to lead them to safety. By the end of the trek she was near death, but eventually Aylward recovered and began ministering to the thousands of refugees that were pouring in from around the country.[56]

Gladys Aylward's life became a map that inspired others to leave the comfort and security of their homes and travel to unknown lands to share God's Truth with the lost. She bravely pioneered uncharted territory and beckoned her fellow explorers to follow in her footsteps. And when they saw the powerful trail she had blazed for them, they too gained the strength to risk their own safety and comfort for their true King.

Becoming a Mapmaker

From Polycarp to Tyndale to Aylward, God's real-life action heroes throughout history have paved the way for future generations to discover the endless frontier of God's grace. They were mapmakers. They didn't wait for someone else to blaze the trail; they were willing to forge ahead into the unknown, trusting the Master Frontiersman to be their guide. They ignored the voices of human wisdom and reason and listened only to the beckoning whisper of Christ.

These were mere mortals, yet the lives of God's mapmakers majestically display the awe-inspiring power of God. Their stories are more action packed and exciting than the most thrilling Hollywood blockbusters. We must remember these heroic lives, because they serve as a heavenly atlas, pointing us toward the narrow path of greatness.

They were simple men and women who lived large on the pages of history, who "by faith conquered kingdoms, performed acts of righteousness, obtained promises, shut the mouths of lions, quenched the power of fire, escaped the edge of the sword, from weakness were made strong, became mighty in war, put foreign armies to flight."[57]

Who wouldn't want such an electrifying existence? Most of us long to make an impact on this world, just as Polycarp, Tyndale, Aylward, and so many others have done. But before we can join the ranks of God's mapmakers, we must first understand the cost.

Making a map means courageously exploring untamed lands. It means giving up everything, even our very life, to follow Christ into the treacherous unknown. It means going past the point of human reason, comfort, and security in order to manifest God's earth-shaking power. It means tackling the impossible, relying on nothing and no one but the Spirit of God to help us make the climb. And often, it means suffering and dying along the way, so that God's amazing love can be displayed to the world through our sacrifice.

God's mapmakers do not typically live wealthy, healthy, and comfortable lives, at peace with the rest of the world. The Bible says that God's action heroes of old faced "[torture]…mockings and scourgings…chains and imprisonment. They were stoned, they were sawn in two, they were tempted, they were put to death with the sword; they went about in sheepskins, in goatskins, being destitute, afflicted, ill-treated…wandering in deserts and mountains and caves and holes in the ground."[58]

It's hard to imagine anything more horrific than the trials these men and women faced. And yet if we truly desire to become God's mapmakers, the consequences we face might be just as severe. But are we willing to give up our very life to follow God into His endless frontier?

In the modern church, there is a prevailing mind-set that we can "have our cake and eat it, too." We think that we can live self-ruled lives full of comfort and ease and still see God do incredible things through us. We think that we can blend God's purpose for our lives into our own self-constructed agendas. We think that we can have everything we want in life and still be a powerful example of Christ to the world around us.

But only when we give up *all* our rights and plans and allow Christ to build our *entire existence* can God transform us into the real-life action heroes we are called to be. Only when we are willing to suffer torture, affliction, and death for His sake can we truly be His representatives to this world.

We may long to experience God's grand adventure, but are we willing to set aside our self-built agendas and yield to His Spirit, no matter what He calls us to do? The Christ-built life is the most thrilling and satisfying existence of all. It is also the most dangerous journey we will ever embark upon. And before our life can become a map for others to follow, we must first count the cost.

True Leadership

Gavin is a young college graduate who squirms at the idea of becoming a mapmaker. "I don't think I'm called to be a leader," he told us. "I took a test to determine my spiritual gifts and discovered I'm more of a behind-the-scenes person."

Brandi is a twenty-one-year-old who lacks the confidence to share the Truth with others. "I'm a really shy person," she says sheepishly. "I want to go into some kind of ministry, but nothing that requires me to talk to people I don't know."

When we hear the challenge to become God's mapmakers, many of us instantly retreat from the idea because we don't feel "called to be a leader." Those of us who aren't confident around people generally assume that we weren't meant for leadership. We believe that we haven't been given the right personality or spiritual gifts to lead others into God's endless frontier.

And then there are those of us who feel extremely confident in our leadership abilities. Take Zach, a fiery young evangelist-in-the-making. "I can't stand not being in charge," he told us with a laugh. "I feel the most alive when I'm up in front of a big group of people. God has called me to have my own ministry, and I know it's gonna be huge!"

But the truth is, Zach is no more called to be a spiritual mapmaker than either Gavin or Brandi. Becoming an effective mapmaker has little do with our personality, spiritual gifts, or confidence in our abilities. In fact, throughout history God's mapmakers have often been the most *unlikely* people to pave the way of Truth for future generations.

David was a lowly shepherd boy, the weakest and youngest of all his brothers. And yet he slew the biggest giant in the land and became the greatest king of Israel. Mary was a poor teenager from a small town who gave birth in a dirty stable. And yet she nurtured and mothered the Savior of the world.

Every one of us is called by God to be a leader, a champion of His Truth to this world. Being a leader for God doesn't always mean writing inspirational books or eloquently preaching to large crowds. Rather, it means giving our lives completely over to the Spirit of God and letting His power shine through us in whatever way He chooses. Our personality, spiritual gifts, confidence, and talents—these things do not make our lives into maps for others to follow. It is the way we allow Christ to live through us that transforms us into world changers.

Putting It into Action

Do you see yourself as anything *but* a leader? Allow God's Spirit to overtake your entire being, and your life will make an eternal impact upon this world whether you open your mouth or not. Don't be stunted by your perception of your personality or spiritual gifts. God will give you the supernatural strength and courage to boldly tackle any challenge He calls you to.

Do you feel confident in your leadership skills? Don't rely on your own abilities to help you impact this world. Instead, let God's Spirit work through your being, and whether you speak before millions or comfort one small child, His Truth will shine through your life. Be willing to become a servant; only then will you be a true leader.

Don't Seek the Approval of Others

Emily is a college sophomore who has recently made the decision to give her love life to God. The only problem is, she doesn't want anyone else to know it. "How do I live in purity without looking like a total prude?" she wrote in a recent e-mail.

The answer to Emily's question is one that she probably doesn't want to hear: *Be willing to appear a fool for Christ's sake.* A God-scripted life is one that inevitably looks strange to those around us. As you make decisions to build your life around Him, don't expect others to understand and approve of your life. God's mapmakers are not deterred by what other people think. Amy Carmichael wrote, "If the praise of others elates me, or if the blame of others depresses me, then I know nothing of Calvary love."[59]

As you allow God to shape you into a mapmaker for Him, don't dwell upon the approval or criticism of others. Instead, fix your eyes on Christ and live for His smile alone.

Let Christ Be the Attraction

As modern Christians, we often go out of our way to make our faith seem appealing to the outside world. We spice up evangelistic outreaches with rock concerts and laser light shows. To prevent boredom in church, we show movie clips, provide entertaining music, and turn our sermons into stand-up comedy routines.

A church in our area recently posted a huge sign near the highway offering free hot dogs and beer to anyone who came to their evangelistic service. The service consisted of an hour of live non-Christian music and a three-minute message about God's love.

God's mapmakers rely on Christ, not cheap human tricks, to draw people to the Truth.

R. A. Torrey was a passionate preacher in the early twentieth century. At one point in his ministry, he felt God calling him to hold revival meetings at the Royal Albert Hall in London, an auditorium that held twelve thousand people. Torrey booked the auditorium in advance, planning to hold a meeting there every night for two months. The preacher whom Torrey had asked to speak at the meetings was not especially talented; he had no gift of humor or wit. And Torrey refused to use the performance of a famous opera singer or circus act to draw crowds, as many other evangelists were fond of doing at the time.

A reporter caught wind of Torrey's plans and came to him in astonishment. "This is the biggest hall in London," he told Torrey. "Not even the most popular singers or speakers can fill this place for two weeks! How do you expect to fill it for two whole months?"

"Watch and see," replied Torrey with a smile.

And sure enough, each and every night for two months, the auditorium was not only filled to capacity, but thousands stood outside, even when it was pouring rain, hoping for a seat. When asked the secret of his incredible success, Torrey repeated the words of Christ: "If I be lifted up, I will draw all men unto Myself."

The simple, undiluted message of Christ crucified attracted the people in droves, not human talent or free food. "It is Christ crucified that draws [people]," Torrey wrote. "It is Christ crucified who meets the deepest needs of the heart of all mankind."[60]

Don't be tempted to use human tactics, trinkets, and trivial things to make the Truth more appealing to the world. Simply share the undiluted message of Christ with both your words and your actions, and you will become a map that leads others to eternal life.

Start Where You Can Today

Geoff is a twenty-five-year-old Christian who wants to make a difference in this world. The problem is, he has no idea where to begin. "I don't see very many opportunities to pour my life out for Christ," he confessed. "How can I fight His battles if there are no battles around me to fight?"

Since we don't live in a country where Christians are persecuted for their faith, we aren't often met with opportunities to sacrifice our life's breath for Christ. Christians in America still enjoy the freedom to worship as they please. And as a result, we may not see clear-cut battles for the Truth looming on the horizon. We want to charge into the fray of God's holy fight, but we don't see a fray to charge into.

Yet though we may not ever have the chance to become

martyrs like Polycarp or Tyndale, we can become *living sacri-fices* for our Lord. How? By taking a closer look at the divine opportunities God has placed in our lives, then allowing God to display His love and power through us in those situations.

Take some time to evaluate the mapmaking opportunities in your life. Do you have a difficult brother or sister? How can you sacrificially show Christ's love in that relationship? Your investment in a sibling's life could be the difference between failure and success for him or her.

Are you a young woman with a passion for mentoring younger girls? Ask God to show you some girls who need a role model, and then initiate a regular get-together or Bible study with them.

Are you a young man with a heart for the homeless? Begin volunteering at shelters and food centers, asking God to showcase His love to the people you interact with.

Opportunities to pour out our lives for Christ are all around us. All we need do is ask God to open our eyes to them—and be willing to sacrifice our own comfort and agendas to allow Him to work through us.

Another thing to prayerfully consider is whether God might be calling you to go somewhere for Him. There are orphanages in Romania that need workers, homeless families in Mexico that need houses built, and unsaved students in China that need English teachers.

Even in America there are many places we can go to pour out our lives in service for Christ. There are prison inmates in need of the gospel, inner-city children in need of tutors, and hospital patients in need of a friend. We recently heard about two young men who spent three months living among the homeless in several cities across the nation in order to share the love of Christ with these forgotten people.

Be willing to leave behind what is comfortable and familiar in order to become a living sacrifice for Christ. God's
mapmakers give no thought to their own desires or security.
Instead, they eagerly spill themselves out as a fragrant offering to heaven.

*God has made me as bread for His chosen ones,
and if it is necessary for me to be ground in the teeth
of lions in order to feed His children,
then blessed be the name of the Lord.*[61]

St. Ignatius, early Christian martyr

In a Nutshell

For a map to be made, a pioneer is needed. Christ was the first pioneer for the superconquering life—He made the map that inspired all the rest. The apostle Paul was a mapmaker. He said, "Imitate me, just as I also imitate Christ."[62] Every generation needs mapmakers, adventurous souls who are first to take the risk, first to ford the dangerous waters, first to be opposed, and first to die for the cause. Every generation is in need of those whose lives demonstrate in living color what can happen with a life fully yielded to God Almighty.

This generation is no different. God is looking for a few willing souls ready to journey into the untamed wilds of His grace. He's looking for a few good pioneers. Who will be the Polycarps, the Tyndales, and the Aylwards of this era?

Could it be you?

Leslie

A GOD-WRITTEN ENDING

*Many people owe the grandeur of their
lives to their tremendous difficulties.*[63]
CHARLES HADDON SPURGEON

Laura has led a difficult life. Her parents divorced when she was three; her father was verbally and physically abusive, and her mother became an alcoholic. Now a young woman, Laura struggles with anger toward God for allowing such heartache into her life. "I want to yield to Christ in every area of my life," she says, "but I'm just not sure I can trust Him. I feel like He's let me down in the past."

A huge majority of our generation has experienced tremendous pain in their lives, from divorced parents to abusive fathers to heart-wrenching romantic disasters. As a result, we are disillusioned with God. Many of us feel that if God truly cared, He wouldn't allow such terrible things to happen in our lives. We have memories of crying out to God for help, only to be met with silence in return. We balk at the thought of turning our entire lives over to a Master who has seemed so indifferent to our pain.

Others have different reasons for hesitating to trust God.

Brian is a nineteen-year-old baseball player who is full of hopes and dreams for his life. He knows which girl he wants to marry and exactly what career path he wants to take. He doesn't want to give those dreams up. And so Brian struggles with the idea of letting God write his life story. "What if I give my life to God and He completely wrecks it?" he wonders nervously.

So many of us have dreams of how we want our life story to turn out. It is easy to think of God as a tyrant who wants to kill those dreams and make us miserable. We often believe that if we hold the pen, we can write a much better ending to our story than God ever could. We fear that if we give our dreams to Him, we will only be hurt and disappointed in the end.

Yet if we were to talk with every real-life action hero who has experienced a God-scripted life adventure, we would hear endless firsthand accounts of God's incredible faithfulness, even when the story did not turn out the way these heroes had planned.

Yes, God sometimes allows great pain into our lives when we give the pen to Him. And yes, God sometimes asks us to sacrifice the dreams and desires we hold most dear. He does this not to make us miserable, but to help us discover even more of His incredible love and grace. Anyone who has ever traveled with Him into this amazing endless frontier will tell you they do not regret, even for a moment, turning their lives over to Him.

Whenever He leads us through difficult times, He is always standing right beside us, offering the grace and strength we need to keep trusting Him. All we need to do is take our eyes off ourselves and our circumstances and look into His loving face. The most powerful demonstrations of God's love and power take place when we choose to implicitly trust Him, even in the face of disappointment, tragedy, and death.

When a man of God named Stephen was being stoned for his faith, he did not focus on the blinding hatred and murderous faces of those mutilating him. He did not beg for his life. The Bible says that he "gazed intently into heaven and saw the glory of God, and Jesus standing at the right hand of God." He was overjoyed to give his life for his King. And as a result, Stephen's death became an incredible demonstration of the triumphant Christian life.[64]

When three young men named Shadrach, Meshach, and Abednego were commanded to bow down to the statue of King Nebuchadnezzar or be burned alive, they chose to trust their God completely, no matter what the outcome. "Our God whom we serve is able to deliver us from the furnace of blazing fire," they said to the king. "But even if He does not, let it be known...that we are not going to serve your gods or worship the golden image that you have set up."[65]

As the three young men were led into the fiery furnace, they did not know whether God would save their lives or allow them to be incinerated. To them it did not matter how the story ended. It only mattered that they obeyed their true King.

When Job was struck with tragedy after tragedy, his wife and friends told him to curse God. But Job chose to leave his life completely in God's hands, even if God decided to take his very life. "Though he slay me, yet will I trust in him," Job declared.[66]

When the young queen Esther knew that God wanted her to go before the king uninvited to make a bold request, she was aware that obeying would likely cost her her life. But Esther was determined to yield to Him, no matter what happened. "I will go to the king, which is against the law," Esther said, "and if I perish, I perish!"[67]

Often we are tempted to yield to God's Spirit only under certain conditions. "As long as You make this love story come together, I will trust You." Or, "As long as You prosper me financially, I will trust You."

But just imagine if Shadrach, Meshach and Abednego had chosen to obey God only if He delivered them from the flames? Or picture Job telling God, "I will only trust You if You give me back everything I have lost." Or what if Queen Esther had demanded that God guarantee her life would be spared before going to see the king?

The only way we can experience a God-scripted adventure is to turn our pen over to the King of all kings with *absolutely no conditions,* allowing Him to write our story in any way He sees fit.

The trek up God's holy mountain will be the most difficult journey of our lives, but remember, it's not we who must do the climbing. It's Him. And He is more than capable of sustaining us through every valley and storm we encounter.

When we entrust our life's pen to the Great Author of Adventure, we can be sure that, come tragedy or triumph, we will experience the most fulfilling story of all time. And no matter what, we can be assured of a happily-ever-after ending—eternity in the presence of our King.

part three

FRONTIER FIELD GUIDE

A Study Guide for Shaping the Inner Life

Men wanted for hazardous journey.
Small wages. Bitter cold.
Long months of complete darkness.
Constant danger. Safe return doubtful...[68]

ADVERTISEMENT POSTED BY ERNEST SHACKLETON, 1914

INTRODUCTION

More than a thousand young men responded to Ernest Shackleton's ad to make the first complete crossing of the antarctic continent. They understood the extreme danger. They knew they might not return alive. But they longed for the adventure of a lifetime, and they were willing to sacrifice comfort and safety to find it.

To discover the heights and depths of God's endless frontier, we must become like Shackleton's men. We must be willing to abandon life as we know it and embark on the rigorous journey that God has waiting for us. The journey begins with shaping our dreams, motives, thoughts, habits, and lifestyle around God's purposes and priorities.

It's easy to talk about living a God-scripted adventure. Living it out in every aspect of our daily existence is another matter. This field guide is designed to help you do just that.

Its purpose is to practically prepare you for the adventure of a lifetime.

The Frontier Field Guide is meant to be a hands-on experience. Please customize this section of the book to your own life as God leads. Work through the material as quickly or slowly as you need to, and concentrate on those areas you feel apply to you specifically. To get the most out of this process, we suggest you set aside uninterrupted time and keep pen and paper available.

It's important to realize that this material is not meant to be a formula. It is vital that you allow God's Spirit to be your Guide during this process—let Him gently shape and mold the areas of your life as He sees fit. Don't embark upon this journey out of self-determination or sense of duty. Pursuing a God-built existence should only flow from a genuine desire to experience the fullness of His Life within you. Your longing for more of Him must be so intense that you are willing to put everything on the line to find what you seek.

The decisions you make as a result of working through this material might look strange to others. Even other Christians might scoff, calling your choices "extreme" or "unnecessary." But remember that every great pioneer, from Lewis and Clark to Ernest Shackleton, once looked foolish to the rest of the world. No matter what the cost, a God-scripted adventure is well worth fighting for.

How to Use This Study

In this section, we have broken the elements of a God-written life into seven critical pieces—the seven landmarks of a God-scripted adventure. Each landmark represents an area of unlimited spiritual growth and potential within your inner life. The goal is not to become a finished product overnight. Rather, simply allow these landmarks to serve as a point of reference for your life's direction, starting today.

This study can be used in a group setting or experienced on an individual basis. If used as a group study, it's still important that you take time to examine each landmark on a personal level, asking God to help you apply the principles to your own life.

To make this material more conducive to group settings, the seven landmarks can presented in a seven-week study, working through one landmark each week. But if you are going through this material on your own, please feel free to work at your own pace. You may find you can work through this material in one sitting, or you may need to break it into sections and spend several days or weeks going through it. The important thing is to be sensitive to God's leading.

At the end of this study is a bonus section called "Cleansing the Inner Life," which is a detailed personal guide to confession and removal of past or present sin in your life. The Cleansing section should be worked through alone or with a godly teammate. During the course of this book, if God has been pointing out to you unresolved sin in your life that is hindering your walk with Christ, you may wish to first work through Cleansing the Inner Life before beginning the Frontier Field Guide.

Leslie and I have worked through this material many times, and each time it has proved wonderfully invigorating to our spiritual lives. We believe it can do the same for you. So without further delay, let's begin the exciting journey of making a God-scripted adventure real and practical in your everyday life!

ADOPTING GOD'S PURPOSE FOR YOUR LIFE

urpose is a buzzword these days. Making purpose statements for our lives, for our businesses, and for our ministries has become quite popular in the modern world. And for good reason. A clear sense of purpose is necessary for a well-lived life. If we don't know why we are here, we don't know what to do with the time we've been given.

But the intrinsic problem with the modern pattern for creating purpose statements is that it relies on merely human wisdom and reasoning. Modern purpose statements focus on what *we* think is important, what *we* deem valuable, and what *we* define as success. As long as you are in the driver's seat of your life, with the pen in your own hand, scribbling out a self-built purpose statement, you will miss out on the *real* purpose for which you are here on this earth.

As lofty as your own goals and dreams may be, they probably still miss the definition of *true success* as defined by heaven. True success is found only when you finally learn to adopt God's purpose statement for your life and relinquish your hold on your own ideas of success. As noble as it may seem, He didn't place us here to "inform every last person on earth about Coca-Cola" or "get a personal computer in every home of every family around the globe." He created us for something much more grand.

We are here on this earth to know God intimately, fully, correctly, and contagiously; to house His holy person in our very bodies, allowing Him to showcase to the world around us His loving nature, His attitude, His thoughts, His emotions, and His actions through the way we live every moment of our lives.

Come up with your own unique way to express God's purpose for your life. The above statement is how Leslie and I say it, but the specific words can, and should be, unique to each of us.

You are here on this earth to simply abide in Him, enjoy Him, and be a vessel for Him to work through to change the world around you. Some might express it by saying, "I'm here to know Him!" Others might declare, "I'm here to abide in Him!" However you choose to phrase it, God's intended purpose and focus for your life comes down to one simple truth: *It's all about Him!*

Staking Claim to the First Landmark

1. Make It Official

Find a place where you can be alone. Bring along pen and paper. Pray and ask God's Spirit to assist you in this process. In your own words, write down the purpose statement that you feel best captures God's desire for your life. Write it in the way that you personally will best understand it. Choose the words that make the most sense to you, so that whenever you read it, you will be clearly reminded of the central focus of your existence.

2. Remind Yourself Often

Place this statement of resolution in a place where you can read it, see it, and meditate on it daily. This statement is what your moment-by-moment life is all about, so come up with creative ways to keep yourself reminded of it. Frame it, post it on the fridge, tape it to your bathroom mirror, write it on your shower stall with a wax pencil, even set your watch to beep on every hour to remind you of this all-important pursuit. The important thing is that you clearly establish this purpose for your life and then work to remind yourself of it every hour of every day until it becomes such a part of you that nothing can tear it away. When God's purpose becomes your purpose, life suddenly makes a whole lot of sense.

Questions for Reflection or Discussion

- What have you always believed your life's purpose to be? Is it different from what God says it should be?

- How have friends, family, and the culture influenced your beliefs about your life's purpose?

- How do you think adopting God's purpose statement could change or benefit your life?

UNDERSTANDING YOUR ROLE IN GOD'S DRAMA

There isn't a human on earth that is an exact replica of another. We have each been perfectly designed and crafted by God for a unique, one-of-a-kind adventure in this life. Some of us are designed to care for orphans, while others are designed to care for hard drives. There are those who are perfectly built for work in the jungles of Africa, and those who have been especially created for work in the jungles of Wall Street. Some of us are designed to stand and speak before powerful rulers, while others are meant to raise the future rulers of this earth.

Even so, our daily and lifelong destination is the same for each of us who claims Christ as our King: to abide in Christ and enjoy our great God. He places us each at a different starting point in this world, at a different time in history, with different obstacles in our way—and then He says, "Come and know Me, My child."

You have been assigned a unique role in God's great dramatic adventure. But before you can understand your role, you must understand your purpose. That is why the first landmark is so critical. Once knowing Him, enjoying Him, and abiding in Him becomes the driving force in each and every moment of your every day, your unique role will begin to become clear.

The role that God has assigned to you cannot and will not be revealed on demand. It's an awakening, an unveiling that takes place over time as you make God your priority.

Still, you can prepare yourself to recognize and understand your role in God's adventure as it emerges in your life. Here are some exercises that can help train your spiritual eyes to recognize the uniqueness of your part in His story.

Staking Claim to the Second Landmark

1. Become Familiar with Heroic Lives

Learn to think like the great Christians that have walked this earth before you. Learn to understand what happens to a life that is completely given over to God. Read their stories. Ponder their lives. Meditate on their impact.

As God's unique role for your life begins to come into view, you may notice that you are facing many of the same challenges, the same tests, and the same struggles they faced. The context of your life is different, but the God orchestrating your adventure is the very same. You will be amazed at how much encouragement comes from knowing that the same God who built these heroic lives is at work within *you* to make your life count in this world.

Here are some great Christian biographies to start with:

Oswald Chambers: Abandoned to God by David McCasland
The Hiding Place by Corrie ten Boom
The Gold Cord by Amy Carmichael
No Compromise: The Life Story of Keith Green by Melody Green and David Hazard
Tortured for Christ by Richard Wurmbrand
Shadow of the Almighty : The Life & Testament of Jim Elliot by Elisabeth Elliot
Through Gates of Splendor by Elisabeth Elliot
They Found the Secret by V. Raymond Edman
Hudson Taylor's Spiritual Secret by Howard and Mary Taylor

These biographies were great inspirations to us in the first years of our relationship and ministry. We can't even begin to describe the impact they have had on our spiritual journey and, ultimately, on our recognizing God's unique role that He has appointed for us.

2. Catch a Vision of What Could Be

One of our favorite spiritual exercises is to ask ourselves, "Which historical figures (other than Christ) best represent the specific attributes I sense God wants to cultivate in my life?"

Does God want you to demonstrate Mother Teresa's poured-out compassion? Hudson Taylor's life of sacrifice on the mission field? Abraham Lincoln's heroic leadership in difficult times?

It may be difficult to answer at this stage of your spiritual growth, but as you become familiar with the lives of those who have gone before you, the answers will start to become clear.

Here's a list of some more heroic lives for you to study: John Wycliffe, Dietrich Bonhoeffer, Rees Howells, Charles Finney, Charles Spurgeon, Harriet Tubman, Florence Nightingale, George Mueller, Esther Ahn Kim, R. A. Torrey, D. L. Moody, Billy Sunday, Gladys Aylward, John Wesley, John Bunyan, Helen Keller and Annie Sullivan, George Whitefield, and Mary Slessor.

As you read about the trials and triumphs of these men and women, you may be able to better recognize and understand what God is doing in your own life.

3. Identify the Missing Ingredients

Now ask yourself, "Which historical Christians represent the attributes of Christ that are *missing* from my spiritual makeup?"

Maybe you don't possess the tender love for God that Richard Wurmbrand displayed in his life, but you sense that God desires to increase that attribute within your life as He continues to mature you.

Maybe you seriously lack the mighty faith of George Mueller, but you know that God wants to strengthen your faith as your life story unfolds.

When you see Christ lived out heroically in the lives of others, you will develop a picture of what He desires to do within you. And that vision will be a catalyst for these Christlike attributes to become a stunning reality within.

Questions for Reflection or Discussion

• Have you studied the life of someone that has inspired you? If so, what attributes of that person's life and character would you like to see in your own life?

• Have you had a limited view of what God can do through your life? How do you think God might want to expand your vision?

HEAVENLY GOAL-SETTING

While it takes a lifetime to fully understand our unique role in God's great story, you can learn what goals to set for your life, *starting today*. Specific goals are the sweat and tears that make up the substance of a well-lived life and ultimately help set the stage for your unique role to unfold on the pages of history.

If you want to live a life that really counts, you must begin to aim in the right direction this very moment. Then you must learn to continually take small steps toward knowing your King better.

To build a house, you can't just throw a whole bunch of wood, nails, concrete, steel, carpet, and insulation onto an empty piece of land and expect this pile of raw materials to look like a beautiful home. Nails won't pound themselves into the wood, and concrete doesn't pour itself. You must actually work to put all the pieces together. And the work takes time.

There are a lot of little jobs that go into the one big job of building a house. The same is true with knowing and enjoying God for a lifetime. The big job is knowing Him and becoming like Him. But that one big job is only made possible by faithfully carrying out the countless *small* jobs that fill our days. For a great Christian life to take shape, you must actually pick up a hammer and start doing little tasks in obedience to the Master Carpenter.

This means setting small achievable goals that aim you toward a direction and purpose. It means reaching for these smaller goals over and over throughout your lifetime. It means keeping the construction process moving forward, come wind, rain, or shine. You must wake up every morning ready to build, ready to pick up your spiritual hammer.

To live a great life, you must remain focused on the end result, and yet happily do all the little jobs that make up the bigger project.

Let's discuss how to set the right kind of goals so that the construction of the Christ-life within our souls is a constant and ever-growing process. To do this, we need to divide life into six key components: 1) the *spiritual* side, the part of our being in which God actually lives and relates with us; 2) the *physical* side, the part of our being that provides practical hands and feet to our life; 3) the *emotional* side, the part of our being that feels; 4) the *social* side, the part of our being that relates to the world around us; 5) the *intellectual* side, the part of our being that contains and develops our thoughts and ideas; and 6) the *ability* side, the part of our being that houses our unique talents and skills.

Each of these six areas is important to the construction of a well-crafted Christian life. So when you set goals for our life, each of these six areas must be considered. Let's look at them individually.

Setting Spiritual Goals

Our spiritual life needs constant forward movement in order to remain healthy and active. But too often we set goals for our spiritual life that are much too large for us to tackle early in our training. We decide to read through the entire Bible in a month, pray three hours a day, and be still and listen to God for another two hours each night before bed. These are wonderful desires, but they can only be realistically achieved when we break them into small, achievable steps.

So instead of determining to read the entire Bible in a month, start by reading through the book of Luke. Instead of resolving to pray three hours a day, start by talking sincerely to God every time you sit down to a meal or the moment you awake in the morning. Once you accomplish your smaller goals, you can gradually work toward bigger ones. There is an endless frontier of possibilities for growth, but great pioneers recognize that the journey must be made one step at a time.

Setting Physical Goals

God sometimes allows sickness into our life to draw us closer to Himself. He allows us to feel physical weakness to remind us of our utter need of Him. So when God brings a physical challenge into our life, we should joyfully embrace it and ask Him to give us the grace to endure.

However, we sometimes create *unnecessary* physical challenges by giving in to laziness or a health-sabotaging lifestyle. We must instead proactively set physical goals to train our bodies toward vitality, not so that we can be confident in ourselves, but so that we can be fully available to our King. Taking care of your body will provide you with the health, energy, and endurance to focus on knowing God and serving Him.

Again, small achievable goals are the key. Instead of setting out to run a marathon next week, start by familiarizing your body with the concept of just getting in shape. Start by adding a salad to tomorrow's menu instead of the chocolate fudge brownie you have your eye on for dessert. Start small, achieve those small goals, then take another small step forward. Olympic athletes are made one training session at a time.

If you have specific physical challenges, ask God to show you how you can turn those challenges into an amazing display of His power, victory, and grace. Instead of allowing your physical limitations to hinder you, make the most of what God has given you and allow His strength to be made perfect in your weakness.

Setting Emotional Goals

God wants to shape our hearts into replicas of His own. To feel what He feels, ache when He aches, and be filled with joy when He is filled with joy. This requires a lifelong shaping of our emotions, in which we train them to revolve less and less around us, and more and more around Him.

His Life, and therefore His love, blooms slowly within us, growing one step of obedience at a time. As we allow Christ to love through us in every situation, His heart grows within us with each act of selflessness and compassion.

In your pursuit to become more like Christ, start by learning to feel what God feels toward your annoying cousin Joey. Or aim at understanding God's heart for a homeless man downtown. A great place to start is with the closest relationships in your life. Learn to feel what God feels for your family members, roommate, or coworkers. Try to feel their pain, patiently endure their unlovely attributes, and love them just the way *He* loves them—unconditionally. With each small step forward in this area, His Life within you will become more and more evident to this world.

Setting Social Goals

God is an expert with people. He always knows exactly what they need. Sometimes they need a tender embrace. Sometimes they just need a listening ear. And sometimes they need a swift kick to the rear end. In every situation, we must learn to respond to people with the amazing patience and love of our God.

Social goals, like all other goals, must be practical and achievable to work. Your first goals may be as simple as smiling more, saying "hello" to people you don't know, initiating conversations, or even looking for ways to encourage your younger brother or sister. Or you might need to try to talk less and listen more, work at becoming more gracious and forgiving, or treat your family members with more courtesy and respect.

Great men and women of God allow Him to transform their selfish habits into Christlike qualities, so that the world can see God shining through them.

Setting Intellectual Goals

To know God and become like Him, our minds must be constantly involved in the pursuit. If the mind becomes stagnant and no longer thirsts for a deeper understanding of God, all the other areas of our being start to shrivel up and die.

To learn is one of the most incredible privileges we, as humans, possess. There is no limit to the growth and development our minds can experience. But a Christ-built mind does not hunger for information and knowledge of this world merely to impress people and garner respect. Rather, Christ-built minds seek knowledge and understanding of God and His creation so that we can more effectively communicate His Truth and His thoughts to a world in desperate need of Him.

Again, it is important to set small achievable goals for growth in this area. Don't concern yourself with what others think you should know. The real question is, What do you need to know to be a useful instrument for God to work through and to live a life fully yielded to Him?

Setting Ability Goals

Some of the goals you set for your life will center around that specific role you are called to play in God's drama.

For instance, if you are designed by God to write books, then you will need to cultivate the ability to write. Once again, learning to write well involves a lifetime of training and must be broken down into a series of steps that carry you toward your destination. You must gain a grasp of grammar and spelling, develop a strong vocabulary, learn how to do research, and even learn to type. And that's just the foundation. A writer cannot expect to be a finished product at the age of sixteen. But with time, discipline, and patience, a great ability can be honed.

If God has constructed you to be a musician, you must know how to play an instrument. A soldier must know how to shoot a gun accurately. If God has designed you for public office, you must learn to speak in public, reason on your feet, make decisions in a crisis situation, and sit through long boring speeches without nodding off.

However God directs your life, you will need to set specific goals to hone your abilities in preparation for the great adventure He has put you on this earth to live out.

Staking Claim to the Third Landmark

1. Take Time to Set Some God-Designed Goals

Goal setting can give you a tremendous sense of purpose, as well as creating forward momentum in your walk with Christ.

Start small and start simple. Don't try to bite off more than you can chew. When you are first starting to set goals, the key is to achieve them.

For each of the six areas of life mentioned above, come up with a defined goal. We encourage you to write each of them down so that you can look at them often. Begin doing this as soon as you are able. Every few months, read through your goals to evaluate your progress. Then set new and higher destinations for your life.

2. Rising After You Fall

If you find yourself getting distracted from your goals and losing momentum, don't beat yourself up. Just get right back up and moving again in the direction of knowing your King.

There are times when life throws us a curveball and knocks us off our game. The enemy of our souls loves to see us off balance and distracted from our real purpose. When such challenges arise—and they will—don't panic or moan about it. Just turn your eyes toward heaven and begin moving toward your goals once again, starting today.

Brother Lawrence made it his life's pursuit to live in the presence of God each moment of the day. Whenever he had finished a task, he examined himself to evaluate whether he had done it while abiding completely in God's presence. If so, he gave thanks to God. If not, he asked God's forgiveness, and "without being discouraged, he set his mind right again, and continued his exercise of the presence of God as if he had never deviated from it." Brother Lawrence referred to this as "rising after his falls" and believed that this attitude greatly helped him grow closer and closer to God throughout his life.[69]

Questions for Reflection or Discussion

- Think of a goal you have set and achieved. In what ways did the experience change or benefit your life?

- When you think of setting goals, do you become excited or intimidated? Why?

- What kinds of things typically stop you from setting or achieving goals? How can God help you to overcome those obstacles?

DEVELOPING HOLY HABITS

All of us have formed habits that dictate the way we live. Our day may start out with the alarm clock beeping at 6 a.m., our sleepy finger pushing the snooze button six times until seven o'clock arrives. Then we wake up, brush our teeth, and pour a bowl of the same cereal we've eaten since we were eight. Our lives are full of odd habits—including many we aren't even aware of—that carry us from one part of our day to the next.

Habits define the ebb and flow of our day. They are conditioned responses that we build into our lives subconsciously to help us accomplish the necessities of life. We form habits around how we work, eat, groom ourselves, wear clothes, even how we take out the trash and feed the cat.

Most habits are meaningless to your true purpose. But

there are a few types of habits that greatly affect you and help to define whether you succeed or seriously flop in this life. And so you need to make sure that those routines become holy habits rather than harmful ones. The experts say that it takes the repetition of approximately twenty-eight times for a specific behavior to become a habit. That means that you must go through a *focused process* in order to let go of any harmful habits and replace them with healthy ones.

Let's look at nine important areas in which developing holy habits can help to make your spiritual life healthy and strong.

Thinking Habits

Your mind is a breeding ground for only two kinds of thoughts—those that strengthen the Christ-built life and those that spawn a self-reliant life. Holy thinking habits train your mind to think like Christ thinks. This kind of thinking guards your mind like an army protecting its city from invasion by an enemy power; whereas harmful thinking habits leave your mind unguarded against renegade thoughts, allowing anything and everything to pitch its tent in your mental terrain. Worldly thoughts, left unchecked, can very subtly undermine the power of Truth as the governing force in your life. Get in the habit of testing every thought against God's perspective as revealed in Scripture. Healthy thinking habits will provide a tremendous strength and calmness to your inner life.

Decision-Making Habits

Every key decision you make impacts your life and spiritual health, so keep an eye and ear toward God whenever you come to a fork in the road. Though God may not always give you specific guidance in every situation, a Christ-built life makes you always ready to hear His voice when He speaks. Holy decision-making habits will remind you to always ask the question, "What would bring the most honor to my King in this situation?"

Harmful decision-making habits presume upon God without allowing Him to speak. If we don't turn to Scripture for wisdom, if we don't think to honor God, if we don't give Him the opportunity to give us specific guidance, we quickly remove God from the throne of our lives and recrown *ourselves* as king.

Crisis-Management Habits

God wants you to immediately turn to Him in times of great stress and hand your concerns over to His gracious, sovereign control. No matter what the crisis—whether it is danger, abuse, financial shortage, sickness, or death of a loved one—God desires you to abide in Him every moment of every day. Holy habits in this area breed a life of peace and joy, even amidst the most challenging circumstances. But too often we give into anxiety, fear, and dread as a knee-jerk reaction. When fear and anxiety are given first rights to a soul in crisis, it gives Satan the opportunity to deliver his twisted perspective to our heart and mind and blocks God's comforting, truth-filled perspective on the situation. The secret to handling a crisis is to always let God speak first.

Conflict-Management Habits

In times of relational conflict, make it your habit to initiate reconciliation, forgiveness, and healthy communication. God doesn't want you to run from conflict, but to courageously and humbly do whatever you can to show the love of Christ in any situation. Harmful habits in this area cause us to avoid the strained relationship, run from it, and comfort ourselves by bad-mouthing the individual involved behind his or her back. Even if the conflict is completely a result of the other person's sin, immediately begin looking for ways to bring healing to the relationship.

Eating Habits

The level of control you have over food in your life can often mirror the measure of control you are allowing God to have over your life. Food is a wonderful gift from God, but God never intended eating to be merely a pleasurable activity. Meals are meant to be a daily act of "coming together," breeding healthy relationships and cultivating gratitude toward our Provider. Healthy eating habits include taking advantage of mealtimes to remember God's goodness, His grace, and His supply in our lives. Holy eating habits mean remembering the needs of others and getting to know those around the dinner table in a more intimate way.

Harmful eating habits, on the other hand, cause us to think only about our own needs and wants. Eating can become a form of escape, a self-satisfying activity that helps us to temporarily forget our problems and avoid the areas that we have not relinquished to Christ. When your eating habits aren't guarded, your inner life may be left unprotected to enemy attack. Instead, cultivate holy eating habits and let the Life of Christ grow within.

Spending Habits

Money is a necessary part of life, but it is a powerful force that can easily take control of your existence. Healthy habits in this area include being slow to spend money, wise to invest it, and quick to give it away to those in need. Do you seek after flashy and trendy things, or only those things necessary for a life that showcases the nature of our God? Healthy money habits mean treating every dollar as God's property, asking at every opportunity, "What would God have me do with *His* money?"

Harmful spending habits cause us to build our lives around the pursuit of money—we buy the things we decide we want, then we have to somehow make enough money to pay for all those things. Unhealthy habits can build insurmountable debt, create tight-fisted Christians quick to spend on themselves but slow to give to others, and allow tremendous amounts of unnecessary stress and fear to creep into the heart and mind. God desires you to use money as a servant to His purposes in your life, rather than for money to become your master and definer of your life on this earth.

Time-Management Habits

Time can so easily slip away from us. We need to view time as a treasure and guard it from being treated lightly. Holy habits in this area will help discipline your life around healthy eating, sleeping, and work patterns. And more importantly, healthy time-management habits protect time in each day for your most vital and valuable activities—time with God, time with family and friends, fulfilling goals, ministry, etc. Healthy time management prevents any one area of your life from crowding out the others, giving a vibrant balance to your priorities.

Harmful habits in this area result in a chaotic schedule. Too often we allow selfish whims to dictate our bedtime, wake-up time, mealtimes, and recreation time. Unhealthy time-management habits tend to give priority to "urgent" things that come up—deadlines, doorbells, e-mails, telephone calls—and overlook the truly important things, causing a mountain of excuses to build up between our actual life and our desired life. But when you manage your time properly, you will be free to grow, to relate, to give, and to accomplish amazing things.

Social Habits

We all have distinct patterns in the way we relate to others. Holy social habits mean seeing every person you encounter as super important to your King. Do you treat others as more important than yourself? Do you consider every person worthy of getting to know and understand better? Do your social habits include sharing smiles and making eye contact rather than scowls and avoidance? Do you offer expressions of love and kindness to those you encounter, rather than disinterest and self-absorption?

Harmful social habits cause us to treat others in our life as less important than ourselves, placing an emphasis on *our* needs, *our* story, and *our* life's agenda. Such habits produce poor spiritual eyesight, so that we are unable to see the concerns of others. Harmful social habits fail to display Christ's amazing reality to this world, while holy social habits create a life that is a conduit of His love and grace.

Alone-Time Habits

What you do when you are alone is a barometer for your entire spiritual life. Alone time is one of the great defining factors of your spiritual existence—the habits you form around this time massively impact the rest of your spiritual and practical life on this earth. Holy alone-time habits treat times of solitude as an opportunity given by God Himself for you to grow. And since God has given you the time, then God should be asked if there is anything specific the time should be used for. Even if you don't feel led toward a specific activity, you should have a collection of healthy activities already waiting when private time arrives.

Harmful habits in this area yield to any number of reckless meanderings, mindless activities, and meaningless pursuits. When we are guided by unhealthy habits in this area, we are stunted spiritually, missing out on the boundless adventure of growth and discovery God has for us.

Each of these nine areas presents a practical project for the life desiring more of Christ and less of self. Habits take time to form. The sooner you begin, the sooner you can experience the richness of an existence that cultivates the things Christ loves and protects against the things Christ hates.

Staking Claim to the Fourth Landmark

1. Set Small Achievable "Habit Goals"

In each of the nine habit areas, set a realistic and achievable goal and begin to condition yourself for spiritual success rather than disaster. Start today and begin to rid yourself of any harmful habits and replace them with holy ones. Do you have a habit of oversleeping? Tomorrow wake up early and take the first step toward developing a new morning routine. Are you habitually critical of others? Make it your goal to encourage at least one person today and start building a new trend in this area of your life. Do you spend money unwisely? Today, purposely pass by something you want and begin training yourself toward a new approach to financial management. Remember, it takes time to develop a habit. Healthy habit changes may be uncomfortable at first, but with time and consistency they will soon become second nature to you.

2. Don't Be Discouraged by Difficulty

Unhealthy habits are hard to give up—your flesh will hold on to them like a bulldog around an ankle. But in those times of challenge, allow God to give you the strength to keep going, to take that one small step forward in the direction of change. If our life in Christ depended on our own willpower, we would all miserably fail. *But it doesn't!* Rather, our life in Him depends on His ability to do what we never could on our own. In those moments of weakness, lean all the more on His strength and ask Him to carry you forward.

Questions for Reflection or Discussion

- Think of some of your most harmful habits. How do you think these habits have affected your spiritual life?

- Think of some of your healthier habits. How do you think these habits have affected your spiritual life?

- What specific techniques, if any, have worked for you in breaking bad habits and/or establishing healthy habits in your life?

CREATING AN ENVIRONMENT FOR SUCCESS

There are certain things in life that, in order to reach their fullest degree of quality, must have the right environment in which to prosper. A flower must have consistent moisture, sunlight, and protection from the more severe elements to become all that it can possibly be. An orchestra must have a concert hall, perfect acoustics, highly skilled players, and a well-trained conductor to bring out the full beauty of a Mozart composition.

The same is true of our Christian lives—it takes a certain kind of environment to cultivate intimacy with Christ and with others. As you nurture this environment, it will breed fullness and success in your life.

Let's discuss the six major elements of a healthy life environment and what makes each one important.

Order

Our God is a God of order, and He desires to bring order to your entire life as well. When your life lacks boundaries, organization, and focus, you can become weighed down with unnecessary concerns and spin in circles, accomplishing very little of substance. But a well-ordered life will thrive with amazing freedom and accomplish more of value in a day than most people do all week. An ordered life isn't stiff and consumed by schedules, but is full of joy, free to give 100 percent in every situation. An ordered life is flexible yet focused, available to meet the demands of the moment but still aimed toward a clear goal. Having an ordered life takes effort and isn't always comfortable, but it creates the security of knowing that the important things are being preserved and emphasized daily.

Do you have a chaotic schedule that causes you to fritter away your hours on meaningless activities? Is your home environment so messy that you can't find your Bible? Are your finances in such disarray that you miss bill payments or remain in a state of constant debt? Let God's Spirit gently reveal the things in your life that need some focus, and then begin to tackle them one step at a time. If you have an especially hard time with organizing certain areas of your life, you may want to consider enlisting the help of an outside person—for example, recruiting an organized friend to help you develop a system for keeping an orderly home.

Calm

A rowdy and rambunctious atmosphere produces stress, while a peaceful atmosphere rejuvenates the body and spirit.

Calmness doesn't mean the absence of activity, but rather the clear reality of God being in control at all times. When your lifestyle is built around placid calm, you cannot be ruffled by life's challenges and unexpected circumstances. When your life is intent on abiding in Christ every moment of every day, you will know a calmness that is overwhelmingly beautiful to the soul. Life will throw you curveballs; it's an inevitable part of living. Bad news may arrive in the mail, an abusive voice may berate you, or sickness may overtake you or a loved one. But if you have the clear understanding that Christ is there at that very moment and in complete control of the situation, you have access to the most perfect peace at the moment of your most desperate need.

To build your life around Christ's calm is a decision that flies in the face of our busy American culture. Everything about this world we live in is chaotic and fast paced; but everything about God is ordered and patient. To cultivate His presence, you must create an atmosphere in your life that resembles His presence. Ask God to reveal to you which areas of your life need to be transformed by His supernatural calm. Do you need to change the way you react to stress? Learn to immediately trust Him when bad news hits? Slow down your overall pace of life in order to more clearly hear His whisper? When you build your life around His perfect peace, nothing will be able to shake you again.

Sanctuary

Even though you may be used to the feeling of being constantly surrounded by people, a healthy life demands a degree of aloneness. You need a sanctuary in your life that you can escape to—a quiet place where you can think, meditate, study, pray, and be still. Privacy, while it may be awkward for some, is a necessary tool for cultivating intimacy with God. Having a sanctuary doesn't require living alone; it just means that you find periodic times to be alone. Privacy makes marriages grow, family relationships flourish, friendships blossom, and our relationship with God bloom. Whether you find your place of retreat outside near the big oak tree or in the farthest corner of your bedroom closet, do whatever you must do to find a way to bring an element of privacy to each and every day of your life.

Love

Thinking only of yourself will breed spiritual disaster. To live a healthy God-built life, practical, selfless love must be woven into the very fabric of your daily lifestyle. You must allow yourself to be open to intrusion and inconvenience, available to help others and willing to assist those in need. Ask God to show you how you can be ready at every moment to demonstrate His great love.

A love-focused lifestyle is revolutionary to this world. It thinks of others first and how to creatively meet their needs. It watches for God to bring people across our path whom we can encourage, assist, pray for, and share the good news of Christ with. When love is a part of our lifestyle, we don't need to pray about whether to help someone or not; we automatically recognize when God is giving us an opportunity to showcase His amazing grace.

Often, we overlook the opportunities to show love right in our own homes. We dream of bringing Christ's love to orphans overseas or street kids in Chicago, the whole while treating the people closest to us with cutting remarks and disrespect. Family members and roommates are an excellent training ground for a love-focused lifestyle. Ask God to show you how you can begin to love them, even in little ways. Does your brother need a few words of encouragement? Does your mom need a hug of appreciation? Does your roommate need help washing his car? Little acts of love can go a long way toward weaving Christ's nature into the fabric of your life.

Laughter

Healthy humor provides refreshment to the soul and health to the body. When you know how to laugh, you know how to live. Life is full of serious problems, but a victorious life looks at circumstances through God's eyes. When you have a heavenly perspective on things, you are calm and confident, living with a smile, no matter how impossible the current situation seems. A lifestyle built around laughter doesn't always laugh outwardly, and doesn't need to focus on the humorous side of life at every turn. But when you learn to accent the serious edges of life with a touch of holy laughter, it adds buoyancy and sweetness to each day. Ask God to teach you how to laugh the way He laughs. His sense of humor is evident in His creation. If you don't believe us, just go to the zoo and observe the hippos or monkeys for a few minutes. Or watch the facial expressions of a baby tasting chocolate cake for the first time. Life becomes full of zest when you learn to enjoy God-given laughter.

Purity

A healthy and holy lifestyle must be kept pure from the stain of the world. So often we as Christians participate in the very same activities the world does and, therefore, reap the same results in our lives. But a Christ-written existence builds a personal lifestyle around activities that are noble, admirable, and honoring to our King. A Christian should enjoy life, but his or her enjoyment should flow from a different source than that of the world.

As others look at your life, they should see a life that is totally devoted and dedicated to our Lord Jesus. Philippians 4:8 tells us to let our minds dwell on things that are noble, right, lovely, pure, and praiseworthy. That's a great test for the influences you allow in your life. Next time you sit down to read a magazine, listen to music, or watch a movie, take a moment to evaluate what kind of influence it will have on the purity of your heart and mind. Does it cause you to dwell on what is pure and excellent, or what is immoral and debased? When you build your lifestyle around godly things, purity will be the natural outflow of your existence.

Staking Claim to the Fifth Landmark

1. Be Willing to Overhaul Your Existing Lifestyle

For most of us, change is not a pleasant thing. But change is necessary if we are to go forward with God. Evaluate your current lifestyle before God and allow Him to show you the areas that must change in order for you to grow in Him.

2. Write a Purpose Statement for Your Lifestyle

A great way to facilitate the growth process is to develop a clear vision of where it is God wants you to go. Earlier, we discussed writing a purpose statement for your overall life. Here, we would like to encourage you to write a purpose statement specifically for your *lifestyle*, the daily atmosphere in which your life with Christ is nurtured and grown. Your statement can be simple or profound, but the key is to clearly capture what God desires your life to look like on a daily basis.

For example, our "lifestyle" purpose statement reads:

> To abide in Him every moment of every day. Waking up each morning with a desire to share our lives with Him and share His Life with others. Expectant to see Him create opportunities in each day to know Him more, enjoy Him more, and serve Him more. Allowing every aspect of our lives to showcase His order, His creativity, and His zest for Life.

Our lifestyle seems quite strange to some people, but that is because we strive to build it around God's priorities and not the world's priorities.

Even if you are in a situation where someone else controls your living environment, you can still determine to create a Christlike atmosphere within your inner life. Do whatever it takes, in whatever way you can, to allow God to have control over the style with which you live your life.

Questions for Reflection or Discussion

- What one word best describes your current lifestyle?

- What one word would you most desire to describe your future lifestyle?

- What are the biggest changes you need to make to your lifestyle in order to create an environment for successful living?

ACQUIRING THE TOOLS FOR BUILDING MOMENTUM

Maybe you want to construct a life that honors and reflects Jesus Christ, but you don't feel you have the necessary tools to make it happen.

You've been told to study your Bible, but where do you start?

You've been told to pray more, but how does prayer actually work?

You've been told to have a daily quiet time, but what does that really mean?

You've been told to love Christ and show His love to others, but how exactly are you supposed to go about it?

Great Christians are not born; they are trained. From sculptors to soccer players to surgeons, every man and woman who hopes to achieve excellence in this world must first learn the basic tools of their trade through study, practice, and hard work.

A guitar player must learn how to play chords and even how to pick or strum before he or she can begin to take strides toward greatness; so too we Christians must be trained in the basic tools of spiritual growth before we can rise to levels of heroism in the heavenly ranks.

Beautiful music doesn't just happen when someone hands you a guitar one day and says, "Figure it out!" A guitarist must first be taught how the guitar works, how to tune it, and how to use it to make noises that are pleasing to the ear. In the same way, our lives can't begin to produce the sweet music of heaven until we first understand the rudimentary elements of the Christ-built life.

Let's look at the basics that we must take time to learn if we are to aspire to be real-life action heroes for Christ. These four basics may seem a bit elementary, but few Christians today have these tools in their spiritual tool chests.

The First Basic: Intimately Understanding the Gospel

This is the very reason we are here, the reason God created us, the reason Jesus Christ came and died for us. It's the amazing message of hope we are meant to share with the world. But ironically, few of us really know what the true gospel is. Following is a brief overview, but I encourage you to dig deeper and study this in Scripture for yourself until the gospel becomes so much a part of you that it defines your very existence.

Part I—Our Design. God designed us to know Him, love Him, abide in Him, and enjoy Him. He built us to spend eternity at His side, intimately sharing the beauties and glories of an eternal existence spent worshiping Him and knowing Him as our Heavenly Lover and Almighty King.

Part II—Our Corruption. But something obstructed this perfect design. Sin crept in and severed the spiritual connection the Creator designed us to share with Himself. God, the rightful ruler of our existence, was removed from power and *we,* little prideful people, crowned ourselves kings of our own lives, thus twisting our souls into a misshapen mess of self-reliance, self-indulgence, and self-absorption. Humankind was quickly brought to the point where it could not help itself out of the bottomless pit it had climbed into, plummeting toward eternal damnation with no way to break its fall. And such is the reality each of us faces when we are born into this world. Though self-assured and unaware of our peril, we all share the same hereditary curse of a sin-ruled life. God is holy and just, and therefore, we must each pay the price for our inner rebellion. And that price is death and eternal separation from God in hell.

Part III—Our Hope. But from the very beginning, God has had a rescue plan in mind. And two thousand years ago that plan unfolded within the small nation of Israel when Jesus was born. God came to earth as a baby, grew up a boy, matured into a man, and lived a human life on earth. He was here for one purpose: *to give us His Life.* He came to demonstrate His great love for each of us, living a spotless existence and sacrificing His spotless Life in place of our own. He died the death *we* were meant to die, and He suffered the penalty for sin that *we* were meant to suffer. In doing so, He broke down the barrier that separates us from God—a barrier that, on our own, we could never overcome. In giving us His Life, Christ also gave us His righteousness. He came to reclaim our souls by offering His Life in exchange for our own.

Part IV—Our Response. Every person must respond to this amazing truth by either rejecting it or accepting it. If you reject it, you are saying, "I want to remain king of my own life, and I'll willingly pay the penalty for my sin." But to accept means to allow His Life to become your own. Which means you give up control of your being and allow Him to regain His rightful throne over your life. And when His Life becomes your own, the death He died becomes *your* death to sin; the penalty He paid for you cleanses your soul and makes your guilty conscience white as snow. He both forgives you *and* empowers you to live a victorious new life. He invades your being, takes up residence in your soul, and takes the pen of your existence to write your life story. And as you protect and preserve His Life within you, His nature will become more and more evident in the way you think, the way you feel, the way you behave, and the way you live. The gospel message is the world-altering Truth of God that must never be diluted or compromised, for within it is the unmatched beauty of a fulfilled and successful life here on earth and for all eternity.

The Second Basic: Intimately Understanding the Attributes of God

To know God, we must learn who He is, how He feels, how He thinks, and even how He acts. God is not at all like us in nature. He is completely "other than" us; or as the Bible says, God is *holy*. He is without fault, perfect in every way.

He is eternal, meaning He has no beginning and no end—He has always been and will always continue to be. He knows everything, is everywhere, and is in control of every detail from the workings of the infinitesimal quark to the movement of every star in every galaxy. But though He is all-powerful and could destroy the entire universe with a single glance, He is Love itself.

He is perfect peace, amazing grace, matchless joy, marvelous mercy, and boundless kindness. But though He tenderly and graciously lifted us from the jaws of destruction, He is a God of fierce fire and holy wrath. He hates sin and cannot, no matter the pain to our lives, allow it to remain in our souls. He is the truest justice, the most excellent righteousness, and the purest goodness. He is majestically patient, perfectly faithful, and passionately in love with His children.

He is more beautiful, more powerful, and more wonderful than any description that could possibly be mustered with the limited vocabulary of human beings. And such is the God we have only begun to know.

If you spend your lifetime becoming acquainted with the marvelous and breathtaking attributes of our amazing God, you will not have wasted even the smallest moment of time. It's a pursuit that will never end, even throughout eternity.

The Third Basic: Intimately Understanding the Promises of God

When you know God's promises, you know you can trust Him and what to expect from Him. The Bible is full of God's many promises to His children. Here are a few of our favorites.

He's promised to never leave us or forsake us (Joshua 1:5; Matthew 28:20).

He's promised to forgive us of our sins and cleanse us from unrighteousness if we ask Him to (1 John 1:9).

He's promised to give us the power to overcome sin, if we trust Him for victory (Romans 6:5–14).

He's promised to finish the work He has begun in us (Philippians 1:6).

He's promised to protect everything we entrust to Him (2 Timothy 1:12).

He's promised to direct our steps if we allow Him to lead (Proverbs 3:5–6).

He's promised to instruct us in the way we should go in this life; He promises to counsel and watch over us (Psalm 32:8).

He's promised to return someday to bring His children home to be with Him in heaven (Acts 1:11; Hebrews 9:28).

Understanding God's promises is one of the most important tools needed for the construction of both a Christ-built life and a heroic Christian existence. As you learn to take God at His Word, His faithfulness will become powerfully evident, and your life will become a supernatural display of God at work.

The Fourth Basic: Practicing the Presence of God

Enjoying an ongoing relationship with Christ every moment of every day requires discipline of both the body and the mind—to constantly be aware of His presence as you brush your teeth, eat your breakfast, get dressed for your day, interact with others, do your daily tasks, and lie down in bed at night. Jesus called it abiding in Him. It means leaning upon His strength every moment and allowing His grace to shape you more into His likeness during every scene of life's drama.

Practicing God's presence is a tool every heroic Christian must carry in his or her spiritual tool belt. It takes a lifetime to master the use of this precious tool, but it is available to you today. We encourage you to begin putting it into practice this very hour, this very minute. Ask God to teach you to abide in Him, to remain focused on Him through the challenges and distractions found in every day.

You could live a fulfilled and world-altering life using just these four basic tools. But these tools represent the mere beginning of where we could go in this endless frontier of knowing our God and being shaped into His likeness. Let's quickly look at some of the other tools that God enjoys cultivating in the lives of heroes-in-the-making:

- Rightly handling the Word of God
- Praying and talking to God
- Being still and listening to God
- Practicing the art of biblical meditation
- Speaking the Truth confidently and effectively
- Communicating Christ's love one-on-one with others
- Becoming an expert observer of others so as to better represent Christ's nature to them

Each of these tools can take a lifetime to master, but you can begin using them this very day, even with a basic level of understanding and development. As you grow and mature in your life with Christ, you may find He has other tools He wants to place in your tool chest—for example, leadership skills, money-handling skills, organizational skills—but those listed here will certainly get you started in the right direction.

Staking Claim to the Sixth Landmark

1. Start Building Your Tool Collection

Purchase a three-ring notebook and fill it with writing paper. Divide it into three sections to represent the first three basic tools—understanding the Gospel, understanding the attributes of God, and understanding the promises of God. Then begin to study what the Bible says about the Gospel of Christ—why He came, why He died, and what that means to you and to the world around you. A great place to start is by reading Matthew, Mark, Luke, and John. Write down your findings in the first section of your notebook.

Next, begin to examine Scriptures with the intent of exploring God's nature, His ways, and His character. Write down everything you learn about His attributes in the second section of your notebook. A great place to begin your study of God's attributes is by reading through the Psalms.

Then study every promise of God that you find as you read the Scriptures, and again write down what you learn. God's promises can be found throughout the Bible, but some great books to start with are the Psalms and Proverbs.

Yes, this is basic stuff, but it is supremely important that you have a solid foundation in these areas. Most of us *think* we know and understand who God is, especially if we've grown up in a church environment and heard Bible stories since we were five. But to truly *know* Him—not just know *about* Him—you must claim His Truth as your own.

As for the fourth basic tool, practicing the presence of God, start simple. Focus on cultivating this reality the moment you wake up in the morning and when you go to bed at night. Start adding more and more moments in your day when you purposely remember Christ and freshly surrender your life into His hands.

2. Throw a Tool Party

Instead of the typical bachelor party when we got married, my brother threw me (Eric) a tool party. All the guys showed up in flannel shirts and came bearing gifts of—you guessed it—tools. It was a great idea and a whole lot of fun. When the party ended, I was the proud owner of a shiny new tool chest for fixing things around the house. The tool party transformed me into a very handy man, or at least that was the idea. (Leslie is still not convinced that it worked.)

You don't have to build up your spiritual tool collection all on your own—you can glean from the knowledge and wisdom of others. A great way to strengthen your inner life is to throw yourself a "spiritual tool party." Ask God to bring people into your life who possess the very tools that are missing from your tool chest. Then spend some focused time with them, gleaning from their knowledge, drawing inspiration from their strength, and being motivated by their example.

Questions for Reflection or Discussion

- What specific tools do you need to add to your spiritual tool chest?

- If you were to throw a "spiritual tool party," who are the people in your life you would invite, and why?

- Think of some ways you could help others add tools to their spiritual tool chests.

DISCOVERING THE POWER OF COMMUNITY

Important Note to Study Groups: *This final landmark is best explored on an individual basis. Discussing and evaluating your church community on the level presented in this section may not be appropriate for a group setting. Instead, we encourage each person in the group to take time to explore this landmark privately. We suggest that any group discussion on this point stay focused on the importance of community rather than on evaluating the current church environment.*

The adventure of a lifetime awaits your pursuit. But there is one remaining piece critical to the balanced and effective growth of your spiritual life.

God designed you to be part of a community. In fact, He built each and every one of us to be a small piece of something much bigger than ourselves. The apostle Paul described this something bigger as Christ's body. For instance, my unique role in Christ's drama may be to function as His left pointer finger. Your unique role may be to become His right foot. By ourselves we cannot accomplish much for the kingdom of God. A finger or foot by itself is wimpy and ineffective. God designed us to work together, to join our strength, to compensate for our weaknesses and head out into the endless frontier as a team—His dynamic body at work on this earth.

While it is generally healthy to spend time with nonbelievers, it is vitally important that you have a group of true Christians who can function as your godly support and accountability system. But it's important to be careful who you allow to shape or influence your spiritual life.

If you are not yet plugged into a local church, we have a list of four key elements to look for in a healthy community of believers. The following list is also helpful if you are considering a potential spiritual mentor, prayer partner, or romantic interest.

Direction

Are the people in this church body headed toward a deeper, more intimate relationship with Christ? Are they hungry for more and more of Him every day? Do the Bible and the Spirit of God function as their highest authorities? Are they willing to allow God to convict them and discipline them?

A healthy community of Christ-followers isn't a group of perfect people; but they *are* people headed in the direction of being made perfect by Christ. For a community to be strong, it doesn't have to be finished and mature in the faith, but it must be moving toward maturity. Don't pitch your tent in a settlers' camp, where feel-good sermons and entertaining music are plentiful but forward spiritual movement is nonexistent. Be sure that the believers you join with are earnestly seeking more of God all the time.

Vision

Does this body of Christians believe that God wants His children to be freed from the power of sin and to live victoriously in love and faith? Do they believe that our lives can become glorious displays of Christ's nature, exhibiting His love, joy, peace, patience, kindness, goodness, faithfulness, gentleness and self-control in an ever-increasing measure?

A healthy community of Christians is one that trusts in the power of God. They do not rely on legalistic rules or formulas for a false sense of spiritual success. Rather, they believe God can transform us from weak humans living defeated lives into supernatural demonstrations of His grace, triumphantly declaring the Truth of His kingdom with the way we live each day. Don't pitch your tent with other settlers in the lukewarm realm of compromise and mediocrity. And don't become ensnared by relying on rules and formulas. Be sure that the believers you join with are willing and ready to be made holy, not in their own strength, but by the transforming power of God.

Lifestyle

Do the people in this body take seriously the responsibility of representing Christ to this world? Do they earnestly desire that others would come to know Him? Do their lives, even in small ways, demonstrate the selfless love of God to the world?

A healthy community of believers is one that doesn't just hear the Truth but lives it out. True believers act on the Truth; they don't just philosophize about it. They love and enjoy their God and want others to do the same. They are passionate to protect His Truth and promote it.

The reason so many nonbelievers today are repulsed by Christianity is because they see so much hypocrisy among our ranks. There are too many so-called Christians who speak the Truth with their mouths but allow the slime of the world to permeate their language, actions, appearance, and attitudes. Be sure that those you join reflect the nature of Jesus Christ, not just inside the church walls, but also in the details of their daily lives.

A Healthy Fear of God

Does this body of believers love the things God loves and hate the things God hates? Do their pursuits and priorities dishonor God or bring Him glory? Do they speak reverently of Him? Do they enjoy worshiping Him and expressing to Him their adoration?

A healthy community of Christians recognizes God's greatness. They tremble before His holiness and deeply adore His sweet grace and mercy. They long to please their God in all they do, all they say, with every thought and emotion. They don't treat Christ like a buddy they affectionately slap on the back, but they see Him for who He really is—the King of all kings and the Lord of all lords. They show reverence for Him during prayer, repentance, communion, and worship.

Don't pitch your tent among those who take advantage of God's mercy and forgiveness, engaging in sin thoughtlessly and demanding His blessing without searching their hearts and truly repenting. Do not fall into the contemporary trap of treating Christ as a casual buddy who offers cheap grace. Instead, seek out those who worship Him as the holy, sovereign, almighty, majestic, infinite, eternal King that He is.

Each one of us is a work in progress. We all have our problems, our weaknesses, our lingering selfish and sinful
tendencies. And the same is true with every community of
believers. Remember, the test of a healthy church isn't their
perfection, but their *priority*. Is Christ their life, their hope,
their destination, their salvation, their love, their fulfillment,
and their greatest joy? If so, then their overall direction is
likely to be vibrant and life-giving. And over time, God will
tenderly iron out their wrinkles and gently straighten their
crooked paths. He dearly loves His body, and your life with
Him will only be made stronger when you join together with
other Christ-built believers as you trek through the endless
frontier of a God-scripted adventure.

Staking Claim to the Seventh Landmark

1. Pray for a God-Built Community

If you do not already belong to a community of
Christ-centered believers, then begin to ask God to
show you a healthy body of true Christians that you
can join up with. Ask Him to lead you to people
who will help you flourish in your walk with Him.
The church He has in mind for you may not be right
down the road, but a Christ-constructed group of
spiritual pioneers is worth whatever time it takes to
get together. In countries where Christians are persecuted, many believers risk their very lives just to
gather and strengthen one another in their faith.

Being an active participant in the body of Christ is an invaluable part of spiritual vitality. God wants to orchestrate this vital part of your life, if you will only look to Him and ask for His assistance.

2. Don't Be Hasty to Jump or Join

Don't make quick decisions in regard to your church community. If you are currently in a church, don't immediately jump ship when you have concerns. And if you have just discovered a new group of believers, don't rush into becoming one of the fold. Instead, take a period of focused time to pray about and evaluate the spiritual atmosphere, the direction, the vision, the life, and the passion for God that is evident among this group of people. Ask God's Spirit to lead you in choosing a church community. Being in church doesn't make a believer; being *in Christ* does. So don't hurry the decision. Take great care for your spiritual life and make sure to plant it in good spiritual soil.

Questions for Reflection or Discussion

- What role, if any, has community played in your spiritual life thus far? What role do you feel God wants other Christians to play in your life?

- Are you currently plugged into a God-honoring community? If not, what specific steps can you to take to find one?

FINAL THOUGHTS

A great life is not the result of a formula perfectly followed but rather of a God wholly trusted. This material will only be powerful in your life to the degree that God is allowed to possess your life. Doing the right thing means nothing unless knowing Jesus Christ more intimately is both the beginning and the end of the action. A life spent wholly and completely upon Him is a life wholly and completely satisfied. Settle for nothing less than the fullness of your God.

Remember that the journey into God's endless frontier is a lifelong adventure of growth and discovery. The goal is not to become an instant finished product; the goal is to keep pursuing more of Christ with all our heart, soul, mind, and strength. If you allow Him to write your life story, He will be faithful to shape you more and more into His likeness.

So keep exploring His amazing grace. We serve an incredible God, and His plans for us are beyond anything we could hope or imagine. When we leave the pen in His hands, we will never be disappointed with the story of our lives.

See you out there in the endless frontier!

Settle it forever, that you are to deal directly with the Holy Spirit, and that He is to have the privilege of tying your tongue, or chaining your hand, or closing your eyes, even in ways that He does not seem to do with others. When you are so possessed with the living God that you are pleased and delighted over this peculiar, personal, private, jealous guardianship of the Holy Spirit over your life, then you have found the vestibule of Heaven. [70]

G. D. Watson

CLEANSING THE INNER LIFE

removing the roadblocks to a God-scripted adventure

This bonus section is a detailed guide for the confession and removal of sin—that is, clearing away those things in your inner life that are hindering intimacy with Christ. Because this material is deeply personal, the best way to work through it is prayerfully, before God, on an individual basis.

It is important that you allow God to customize this section for your own unique walk with Him. It can't be made into a formula. The process and results won't be the same for any two people. Invite God's Spirit to guide you through this material, pinpointing the areas in your life that He specifically wants to deal with. Do not enter this process out of a sense of duty, but because of your love for Christ and your desire to experience deeper intimacy with Him.

This is a process that demands an extended, focused effort. You shouldn't feel rushed, but should slowly and thoughtfully walk your way through this section. Have pen and paper ready on which to write down what the Spirit of God stirs within your heart and mind. As you journey through the material, allow His Spirit to bring to your mind things not included in this list. Our God is faithful not to leave any stone unturned.

Be aware that this process won't be easy. Often old wounds must be exposed before true healing can take place. But the freedom that follows is worth the momentary struggle within your heart and mind ten million times over.

Getting the Most from This Process

When we have lived amidst trash for a long time, we grow accustomed to the smell and often forget that the trash is even there. If this is the first time you have ever walked through an inner cleansing process, it can be quite shocking to realize how much junk you have piled up within your soul. Lean heavily upon the strong arm of your King throughout this journey and always remember His amazing love for you. He loves you so much that He will not allow you to remain buried beneath the trash.

To each of these questions you will need to answer *yes* or *no*. There is no use hiding from the truth and acting as if the question doesn't apply to you if it really does. God knows every thought, action, and attitude you have ever had. Trying to justify or reason the garbage away doesn't remove it. Only by answering honestly can you remove the garbage from your inner life and discover the freedom that Christ purchased for you on the cross.

When you answer yes to any question, it is important that you then walk through the following five steps of dealing with the specific sin before God.

Freedom in Five Glorious Steps

1. *Humbly tell God about the specific sin.* Yes, He already knows, but speaking it to God brings it to the surface. Acknowledging your sin to God is like saying, "God, I finally get it! I agree with You! This *was* wrong!"
2. *Ask forgiveness from God.* It's only when you acknowledge the sin and ask Him to wash you clean, based on the merits of Christ's shed blood, that cleansing really can take place.
3. *Turn and walk a new and different way.* The Bible calls this repentance, which simply means a decision to no longer commit that sin. This is not just a feeling of remorse for your sin; it's a practical change of your life so that you don't allow that sin to find its way back into your soul.
4. *Ask God to show you anything else that needs to be done about your specific sin.* If your wrongdoing affected someone else, it is possible that God may want you to go to that person(s) and make things right. If you stole, you may need to repay with interest. If you lied, you may need to set the record straight by telling the truth and attempting to undo the effects of your lie. If you were playing with witchcraft, you maybe need to burn the items associated

with your witchcraft. IMPORTANT: There are a few exceptions to this principle. If your specific sin involved something that you harbored in your mind—like lust, jealousy, or anger—then it is typically *not* appropriate to confess your sin to the person who was the object of your sinful thoughts.

5. *Obey and do what God leads you to do.* Be willing to do whatever it takes to make things right. And when God communicates that you need to do something, *do it!*

Dealing with Those Impacted by Your Sin

If God asks you to personally interact with the individual you wronged, there are three things that are important to remember. First, *acknowledge your wrongdoing and express sincere regret.* Second, *sincerely and humbly apologize and ask their forgiveness for what you did.* But do not make your apology conditional upon receiving the person's forgiveness; it is possible that he or she may choose not to forgive you. Third, *do whatever it takes to make right what you have done wrong.* It's not always possible to right your wrongs, but perhaps there is something you can do, small or large, to express and introduce the love of Christ into a situation or a relationship where you originally displayed the absence of Christ.

REMOVING SINFUL RESIDUE

L et's get started. Remember to take this process slowly. It is better to emphasize quality over quickness in this experience.

Sinful residue lingering within our souls takes on four different appearances:

1. Sinful acts I have committed
2. Christlike acts I did *not* commit
3. Sinful thoughts and attitudes I have had
4. Christlike thoughts and attitudes I did *not* have

We will work through each of these separately.

I. Sinful Acts I Have Committed

For each of these questions, it is important that you write down every incident that comes to mind so that you can deal with each incident individually. Each sin was committed individually, so each sin must also be dealt with individually. Allow God's Spirit to bring to your mind even things that happened when you were a child.

For each sin the Holy Spirit brings to your attention, be sure to walk through the "Freedom in Five Glorious Steps" process detailed on page 205.

Question #1
Have I ever deliberately told a lie about someone in order to injure them?

Question #2
Have I ever exposed someone's faults for the pure enjoyment of seeing them look bad or odd in someone else's eyes?

Question #3
Have I ever made someone feel less important because of how they dressed, how they spoke, how little money they had, the color of their skin, or because I found out that they were unable to help me?

Question #4
Have I ever made someone feel more important simply because of how they dressed, how they spoke, how much money they had, the color of their skin, or because of their ability to help me?

Question #5

Have I ever hurt someone by the way I spoke to them or by the way I treated them? Have I ever verbally or physically harmed someone out of anger or frustration?

Question #6

Have I ever taken revenge on someone for something they did to me? Have I ever "evened the score" by harming someone's life or reputation in some way?

Question #7

Have I ever fought with someone verbally or physically with the intent to hurt them?

Question #8

Have I ever participated in the taking of a life? This may include pressuring someone to have an abortion, consenting to or having an abortion, counseling someone towards suicide, or deliberately (or accidentally) committing murder.

Question #9

Have I ever cheated on a test? Have I ever passed on false information about myself to look better in someone's eyes?

Question #10

Have I ever counted or measured something inaccurately for the purpose of personal gain?

Question #11

Have I ever participated in sexual banter, flirtation, or dirty talk? Have I ever attempted to sexually arouse another person with my speech or physical behavior outside the confines of marriage?

Question #12

Have I ever willfully participated in any mode of sexual touch with another person outside of marriage? Have I ever willfully allowed someone to sexually arouse me? Have I ever touched or observed someone else for the purpose of my own sexual arousal or for the purpose of sexually arousing them?

Question #13

Outside of marriage, have I ever willfully been aroused—by myself or another person—to the point of sexual climax? Have I ever aroused another person to the point of sexual climax outside of marriage?

Question #14

Have I ever willingly looked at pornography of any kind, whether in print, on the Internet, or on television or film? Have I ever participated in creating pornography or in making pornography available to others?

Question #15

Have I ever looked at someone else lustfully? Have I ever created sexual fantasies in my mind?

Question #16

Have I ever used force, coercion, or violence toward someone else for the purpose of my own sexual gratification?

Question #17

Have I ever willfully engaged sexually with anyone or anything outside of the opposite sex? Have I ever willfully engaged sexually with a member of my same sex?

Question #18

Have I ever been immodest? Outside of marriage, have I ever allowed sensuous portions of my body to be seen by the opposite sex? Have I ever deliberately dressed in a manner that might cause the opposite sex to become sexually aroused? Have I allowed my body to be viewed in a manner that would make my future spouse jealous?

Question #19

Have I ever broken a trust? Have I ever knowingly or unknowingly shared something that I promised never to reveal? Have I ever violated a person's trust by doing something that I was asked (or I promised) not to?

Question #20

Have I ever deliberately said, written, or implied something that was not true, for my own selfish gain or for the selfish gain of someone else? Have I ever exaggerated the truth or diminished the truth for my own selfish gain or for the selfish gain of someone else?

Question #21

Have I ever lied to my parents or to anyone else for the purpose of covering up my sinful behavior or for the purpose of protecting my image?

Question #22

Have I ever dishonored my parents? Have I ever shared something about my parents with the intent to lower their reputation in someone else's eyes? Have I ever diminished their good character by behaving poorly in public?

Question #23

Have I ever dishonored an authority figure (teacher, police officer, coach, pastor/youth pastor, political official, employer, etc.)? Have I ever shared something about an authority figure with the intent to lower their reputation in someone else's eyes? Have I ever diminished their good character by behaving poorly in public while representing them?

Question #24

Have I ever been disobedient to my parents? Has there ever been a time when my parents asked me to do something and I either did not obey or was slow to obey?

Question #25

Have I ever been disobedient to God? Has there ever been a time when God was asking me to do something and I either did not obey or was slow to obey?

Question #26

Have I ever stolen? Have I ever taken something from someone else's possession (whether large or small) that I did not buy or was not given?

Question #27

Have I ever willfully allowed myself to fall under the power of a mind-altering substance, be it alcohol or a drug, for the purpose of social acceptance or personal pleasure?

Question #28

Have I ever bragged about myself? Have I ever made mention of my personal accomplishments or my abilities for the purpose of looking better in someone's eyes?

Question #29

Have I ever participated in any evil practices or rituals that honored any power other than Jesus Christ, the God of the Bible? Have I ever allowed another power, outside that of the Holy Spirit, to work through me, speak to me, direct me, or inform me in any way?

Question #30

Have I ever misused God's name? Have I ever behaved in public in any way that would disgrace the name of Jesus Christ? Have I ever spoken in such a manner that the person of Jesus Christ was lessened in another's eyes?

II. Christlike Acts I Did *Not* Commit

For some of these questions, it is not possible to write down each individual incident. For the ones you answer yes to but are unable to remember specific incidents, follow steps 1, 2, and 3 from the "Freedom in Five Glorious Steps" process detailed on page 205. When you are able to remember specific incidents, be sure to walk through each of the five steps.

Question #31

Have I not allowed God's Word to be the determining factor in how I make decisions and live my life, instead trusting in my own reasoning abilities?

Question #32

Have I ever been ungrateful? Has there ever been anything that I have been given, either by another person or by God, for which I did not properly show or express gratitude?

Question #33

Have I ever been stingy with my possessions? Have I ever known of a person's need, had the resources to help them, but chose not to?

Question #34

Have I ever been unhelpful? Have I ever known of someone in need of assistance, been in a position to help them, but chose not to?

Question #35

Have I ever given in to unbelief? Have I ever been in a situation where I allowed my mind to be controlled by fear, anxiety, and foreboding, rather than turning to God, asking for His assistance, and trusting that He is faithful to supply everything I need?

Question #36

Have I ever given in to impatience? Have I ever "given up" on something I was asked to do, simply because the process was either too difficult or not moving fast enough? Have I ever complained about a wait being too long?

Question #37

Have I ever been unkind? Have I ever noticed someone was in need of kindness, but for the sake of my own comfort or reputation, I ignored them?

Question #38

Have I ever had the opportunity to share the Truth of Jesus Christ, but for the sake of my own comfort or reputation, I ignored it?

Question #39

Have I failed to honor my future spouse with the way I have chosen to live my life? Would my future spouse feel jealous, hurt, or unloved by my thoughts and actions?

Question #40

Have I been unwilling to give my every possession over to Jesus, so that I am no longer owner but rather a steward of them? Have I been unwilling to make time with Him the most important thing on my daily agenda? Have I been unwilling to give Him complete access to my bank account? Have I been unwilling to fully entrust Him with my future? Have I been unwilling to give Him all my rights (e.g., the right to be married, to be comfortable and happy, to do things my way)?

III. Sinful Attitudes or Thoughts I Have Had

For some of these questions, it is not possible to write down each individual incident. For the ones you answer yes to but are unable to remember specific incidents, follow steps 1, 2, and 3 from the "Freedom in Five Glorious Steps" process detailed on page 205. When you are able to remember specific incidents, be sure to walk through each of the five steps.

Question #41

Have I ever had jealous thoughts? Have I ever wanted something all for myself that really wasn't mine?

Question #42

Have I ever wanted to switch lives with someone else? Have I ever been mentally consumed by the longing to have something of material value that belonged to someone else?

Question #43

Have I ever complained? Have I ever given in to self-pity?

Question #44

Have I ever been fearful of the future? Have I ever convinced myself that bad things would take place in the next weeks, months, or years of my life?

Question #45

Have I been unforgiving? Is there anyone in my life whom I have never forgiven or refused to forgive?

Question #46

Have I allowed resentment and bitterness into my heart and mind?

Question #47

Have I ever allowed myself to dwell on thoughts that were untrue, perverted, impure, proud, or selfish? Have I allowed my mind to be unguarded, where my thoughts were not checked and filtered, but free to infect my inner life?

Question #48

Have I ever had hateful thoughts toward either God or another person?

Question #49

Have I ever given in to anger and entertained thoughts of destruction toward someone I was angry with?

Question #50

Have I ever felt more important than others? Have I ever thought of anyone as being less important than myself?

IV. Christlike Attitudes or Thoughts I Did *Not* Have

For some of these questions, it is not possible to write down each individual incident. For the ones you answer yes to but are unable to remember specific incidents, follow steps 1, 2, and 3 from the "Freedom in Five Glorious Steps" process detailed on page 205. When you are able to remember specific incidents, be sure to walk through each of the five steps.

Question #51

Have I ever felt apathetic, uninterested, or unloving toward those who do not yet know Jesus Christ?

Question #52

Have I ever felt apathetic, uninterested, or unloving toward my Christian brothers and sisters?

Question #53

Have I been unwilling to sacrifice my personal resources to support those less fortunate than me?

Question #54

Have I been unwilling to look like a fool in order to serve the Lord Jesus Christ?

Question #55

Have I been unwilling to be mistreated, ridiculed, mocked, or falsely accused in order to serve the Lord Jesus Christ?

Question #56

Have I been unwilling to make God's opinion of me more important than the world's opinion?

UPROOTING ALL OTHER MASTERS

I f you have ever surrendered to a master other than Jesus Christ—such as an ungodly attachment or an addiction—you will need to take steps to remove its grip on your inner life. Some of these "other masters" can be yanked out like a weed, but there may be others that will take some time and, potentially, help from another mature Christian(s) to fully remove these attachments from the soil of your heart. We call these "tree stump issues."

There are five categories of "other masters" that may still have a hold on your inner life:

1. Romantic attachments
2. Addictive behaviors
3. Unforgiveness

4. Inordinate affections
5. Ungodly allurements

Let's work through each of these separately:

I. Romantic Attachments

Romantic attachments are insidious things. We derive tremendous pleasure from them for a season, but long after the fling is over, we find that these attachments have glued themselves to our soul and refuse to leave our heart and imagination. For years they can toy with our emotions, pluck at our heartstrings, distract us from our Heavenly Master, and hinder our ability to give ourselves completely to our future spouse. If you have ever participated in any of the following emotionally based activities outside of marriage, it is very possible that you have a romantic attachment taking up space in your inner life that you need to kick out.

"Weed Level" Attachments

If you have participated in any of the following activities, carefully walk through steps 1, 2, and 3 of the "Freedom in Five Glorious Steps" process detailed on page 205. Ask the Holy Spirit to remove any existing attachments and free you from their hold.

1. If I ever cultivated a mental infatuation toward another person
2. If I ever became romantically attached in an emotionally

controlling manner to someone other than a fiancé(e) or spouse

3. If I was ever sexually aroused by another person's words or physical touch outside of marriage

"Tree Stump Level" Attachments

If you have participated in any of the following activities, it may be necessary to involve a biblical counselor in the process of removing these "other lovers" from the soil of your heart. The more that you have given of yourself in a sensually based relationship, the stronger the hold the romantic attachment can have on your heart. First walk through steps 1, 2, and 3 of the "Freedom in Five Glorious Steps" process; then if you sense that a more aggressive tack is necessary, seek out someone who can help walk you through the removal process on a deeper, more personalized level. NOTE: In some situations, God may lead you to also walk through steps 4 and 5 to deal with the romantic attachment. If so, it may be important to gain advice from a professional biblical counselor before you do.

4. If I ever spoke words of commitment to another person who was not my fiancé(e) or spouse
5. If I ever had words of commitment spoken to me by another person who was not my fiancé(e) or spouse
6. If I ever reached sexual climax with the assistance of another person outside of marriage
7. If I participated in repeated sexual encounters with another person outside of marriage

II. Addictive Behaviors

Addictive behaviors can be a challenge to remove. When you develop an addictive behavior, you often don't even realize it. You justify its presence in your life with rationalizations. You tell yourself things like *This is something that everyone does* or *I could give it up anytime I want to* or *After all, doesn't God want me to be happy?*

The telltale sign of an addictive behavior is that it is nearly impossible to let go of. Addictive behaviors take up space in our soul because they provide a false sense of comfort and security, thereby not allowing Christ to provide us with the real thing. Anything that attempts to replace the work of Christ in your life keeps you from discovering the fullness of a relationship with Him. Addictive behaviors, even the seemingly small and insignificant ones, must be kicked out. You will find that some of the behaviors listed below are not sinful in and of themselves; rather, it is the unhealthy and controlling craving for them that is.

"Weed Level" Addictions

If you answer yes to any of the following questions, carefully walk through steps 1, 2, 3, and 5 of the "Freedom in Five Glorious Steps" process detailed on page 205. Ask the Holy Spirit to powerfully break the unhealthy and controlling hold that the addiction has over your life.

8. Has my need for energy and alertness created an unhealthy and controlling craving for any form of caffeine, painkillers, diet supplements, or performance enhancers?

9. Has my need to look perfect physically created an unhealthy and controlling craving for any of the following activities: excessive physical exercise, daily weight observance, inordinate amounts of time in front of the mirror, or a mental preoccupation with what is wrong with my body and how it could be improved?

10. Has my need for a "break from reality" created an unhealthy and controlling craving for any of the following activities: watching television, watching movies, excessive sleeping, reading books or magazines, daydreaming, or listening to music?

11. Has my need to be "popular" created an unhealthy and controlling craving for any of the following activities: being where the party is, always being around friends, staying socially active, making myself the center of attention, or doing whatever it takes to be popular?

12. Has my need for physical comforts created an unhealthy and controlling craving for any of the following items: money, clothes, cars, expensive brand-name merchandise, expensive gadgets, or the unwise use of credit card debt to obtain them?

"Tree Stump Level" Addictions

If you answer yes to any of the following questions, it may be necessary to involve a professional biblical counselor in the process of removing these "other masters" from the terrain of your soul. First walk through steps 1, 2, 3, and 5 of the "Freedom in Five Glorious Steps" process; then if you sense that a more aggressive tack is necessary, seek out someone who can help walk you through the removal process on a deeper, more personalized level.

13. Has my need for "emotional validation" or sensual expression caused me to have a controlling craving for any of the following activities: sexual body contact with another person, experiencing sexual arousal to a point of climax, having sexual imaginings, or viewing pornography?

14. Do I have a controlling craving for personal harm through cutting or self-mutilation (if yes, professional biblical counseling is essential and medical attention is highly advised); or harm toward someone else through physical or verbal abuse (if yes, professional biblical counseling is essential)?

15. Do I have a controlling craving for any of the following activities: displays of anger and/or violence, willful depression, or deliberate physical sickness?

16. Do I have a controlling craving to participate in any of the following activities: excessive eating, nicotine intake, drug use (legal or illegal), or alcohol use?

III. Unforgiveness

Unforgiveness is our way of punishing those who have hurt us. We reason that if we hate them, think evil thoughts about them, resent them, and turn bitter against them, that we will somehow get back at them for all the horrible things that they have done to us. Ironically, unforgiveness rarely accomplishes what we think it accomplishes. Typically, the only thing that happens is that the disease of unforgiveness eats away at our insides and turns our souls black with hate.

For a healthy spiritual life, it is essential that you learn to walk through the process of forgiving someone who has hurt you. Forgiveness is the avenue by which Christ increases in your life. If you block off that avenue with unforgiveness, it will disable you from exploring the endless frontier life with your King.

One of the reasons why many of us struggle in this area is that we have a misconception of what forgiveness really is. Many think that to forgive someone is to forget what he or she did or excuse their wrong. But forgiveness is, in fact, a radical freeing of the soul involving the following three decisions.

Three Critical Decisions of the Will

- *Choosing to take the person's "hook" out of you.* That is, choosing peace instead of bitterness; agreeing to live, from this point on, with the consequences of their sin; and allowing God, as only He can, to turn into good what the enemy meant for evil.
- *Choosing to let this person off your "hook."* That is, being willing to see God forgive and heal this person, and choosing to not hold their sin over them from this point forward.
- *Choosing to put them on God's "hook."* That is, allowing God to deal with the person in His wisdom.

"Weed Level" Unforgiveness

If you answer yes to any of the following questions, for each of the instances and individuals involved, carefully walk through both the "Three Critical Decisions of the Will" and the "Freedom in Five Glorious Steps" process detailed on page 205. As you walk through this emotionally charged process, allow yourself to be honest with your feelings. Ask the Holy Spirit to assist you in taking these important steps forward in your spiritual life.

17. Am I harboring unforgiveness against a family member for doing any of the following: stealing something of material value from me, treating me rudely, ignoring me, causing me discomfort, forgetting me, accidentally injuring me, lying to me, gossiping about me, making me wait, embarrassing me, not assisting me when I needed help, or not showing gratitude to me for something I did to help them?

18. Am I harboring unforgiveness against anyone outside of my family for doing any of the following: stealing something of material value from me, treating me rudely, ignoring me, causing me discomfort, forgetting me, accidentally injuring me, lying to me, gossiping about me, making me wait, embarrassing me, not assisting me when I needed help, or not showing gratitude to me for something I did to help them?

19. Am I harboring unforgiveness against *myself* for doing any of the following: not being good enough, not being smart enough, not being attractive enough, not being talented enough, not being healthy enough, not being likable enough, or not being confident enough?

20. Am I blaming God and, therefore, harboring unforgiveness against Him for not making me smart enough, attractive enough, talented enough, healthy enough, likable enough, or confident enough? Or for not placing me in a better family or life circumstance?

"Tree Stump Level" Unforgiveness

If you answer yes to any of the following questions, the assistance of a biblical counselor in the forgiveness process is highly advised. For each of the instances and individuals involved, carefully walk through both the "Three Critical Decisions of the Will" and the "Freedom in Five Glorious Steps" process. Again, allow yourself to be honest with your feelings. Ask the Holy Spirit to assist you in taking these important steps forward in your spiritual life.

21. Am I harboring unforgiveness against anyone in my family for doing any of the following: intentionally injuring me, verbally abusing me, falsely accusing me, abandoning me, not protecting me, betraying an intimate trust, or sexually violating me (abuse, rape, touching, or looking)?

22. Am I harboring unforgiveness against anyone outside of my family for doing any of the following: intentionally injuring me, falsely accusing me, betraying an intimate trust, or sexually violating me (abuse, rape, touching, looking, or taking advantage)?

23. Am I harboring unforgiveness against myself for doing any of the following: participating in the taking of a life (e.g., pressuring/counseling someone to get an abortion,

having an abortion, murder, assisting in a suicide), injuring someone, sexually violating someone, being sexually violated, or injuring the person of Jesus Christ?

24. Am I blaming God and, therefore, harboring unforgiveness against Him for doing any of the following: allowing sickness or disease into my life or the life of a loved one, allowing the death of someone close to me, allowing extreme challenges into my life, or allowing me or someone else to be abused verbally, physically, or sexually?

IV. Inordinate Affections

If a family you knew was consumed with ham, you might think them a bit strange. If they always thought about ham, sang songs about ham, read books about ham, watched shows about ham, and every time you were around them they talked about ham, you might conclude that this family has an inordinate affection for ham. Ham, in and of itself, is a harmless thing. Yet when it occupies someone's mind to an unhealthy degree, it becomes harmful to the soul of the individual.

Inordinate affections usually surface when you lie down in bed at night. If when you lie down your mind always goes to the same old subject, then it's very possible that you have an inordinate affection in your life.

Your love relationship with your King is the place where God designed your affections to be centered. He intended that you would find complete satisfaction in knowing, loving, and adoring *Him*. Whenever something else captures your heart and your affections, it draws you, very subtly, out of your intimate relationship with Christ. Therefore, inordinate affections must be removed. After all, the first commandment given to Moses was "There shall be no other gods before me." Nothing should ever be allowed to block your worship, love, and adoration from being fully expressed to your Heavenly Master.

Recognizing Inordinate Affections

If you answer yes to any of the following questions, carefully walk through steps 1, 2, and 3 of the "Freedom in Five Glorious Steps" process detailed on page 205. Ask the Holy Spirit to powerfully break the unhealthy and controlling hold that the inordinate affection has over your mind. The key to freedom from these affections is to first recognize they are there. Then it becomes much easier to fight them effectively.

25. Do I find that my mind spends far too much of its focus on any of the following: my outward appearance, my physical health, what other people think about me, anything I said or did, or following the current trends in dress, talk, and behavior?
26. Do I find that my mind spends far too much of its focus on any of the following: looking for what's wrong with others, comparing myself with the way others talk or dress or behave, or looking for what's wrong with me or my life?
27. Do I find that my mind tends to focus on the opposite sex in an unhealthy way? On pondering the opposite sex for unhealthy amounts of time? On wondering if I am liked by certain members of the opposite sex? On imagining myself and certain members of the opposite sex together

as an intimate couple? On imagining members of the opposite sex in a sexually explicit manner?

28. Do I find that my mind spends too much of its focus on any of the following: personal success in some venture (a game, a competition, a performance, a test, a project, etc.) or someone else's success in a similar venture?

29. Do I find that my mind tends to focus on any of the following: things that are imaginary, things that "could be" but aren't, what "could have been" but isn't, things that have never happened "but could," or things that did happen that I wish hadn't?

30. Do I find that my mind tends to focus on things that bring me personal comfort (e.g., sex, drugs, alcohol, nicotine, food, music, money, sports, movies, clothing, cars, gadgets)?

31. Do I find that my mind tends to focus on things that are harmful to me or to others (i.e., violence to myself or to others)? If yes, then please confide in a professional biblical counselor as soon as possible to work through the removal of this inordinate affection.

V. Ungodly Allurements

If you think of the soul as a young puppy, then ungodly allurements would be like chicken bones. Little puppies are extremely attracted to both the smell and the taste of a chicken bone, but a chicken bone can be very dangerous, even deadly, to a young puppy. Ungodly allurements can be extremely attractive but are equally dangerous to our souls. If allowed into the life of a Christian, ungodly allurements will choke out the presence of Christ by, over time, convincing us that building our lives completely around Christ is foolishness.

These are commonly things that we allow into our lives to entertain us, inform us, and bring comfort to us. But if these forms of entertainment, information, and comfort are contrary to the nature of Christ, they must be handled very carefully. When you were two years old, your parents probably told you not to touch the hot stove, not because the stove was a bad thing, but because as a two-year-old you weren't ready yet to know how to make it a useful instrument without getting hurt. Ungodly allurements are similar. After many years of maturing in your love relationship with your King, it is possible to utilize these "allurements" as tools in your hand to help you more effectively reach the world around you for Christ.

However, an ungodly allurement can be transformed into a godly tool only when your mind has been rebuilt by the Spirit of God. At that point, no longer will you look to this "input" as a means of understanding *what* to believe; instead, you will see it as a means of understanding how others are trained to believe and how to possibly reach them.

Recognizing Ungodly Allurements

Look over the following list of potential allurements. Ask the Spirit of God to show you if any of these have had an unhealthy influence on your inner life. If so, carefully walk through steps 1, 2, and 3 of the "Freedom in Five Glorious Steps" process detailed on page 205.

32. Television—Have I allowed television to negatively influence my behavior, my thinking patterns, my sense of

right and wrong, or my attitudes toward God, life, and others?

33. Movies—Have I allowed movies to negatively influence my behavior, my thinking patterns, my sense of right and wrong, or my attitudes toward God, life, and others?

34. Music—Have I allowed music to negatively influence my behavior, my thinking patterns, my sense of right and wrong, or my attitudes toward God, life, and others?

35. Books—Have I allowed books to negatively influence my behavior, my thinking patterns, my sense of right and wrong, or my attitudes toward God, life, and others?

36. Magazines—Have I allowed magazines to negatively influence my behavior, my thinking patterns, my sense of right and wrong, or my attitudes toward God, life, and others?

37. Newspapers—Have I allowed newspapers to negatively influence my behavior, my thinking patterns, my sense of right and wrong, or my attitudes toward God, life, and others?

38. Internet—Have I allowed my activities on the Internet to negatively influence my behavior, my thinking patterns, my sense of right and wrong, or my attitudes toward God, life, and others?

39. Friends—Have I allowed certain friendships in my life to negatively influence my behavior, my thinking patterns, my sense of right and wrong, or my attitudes toward God, life, and others?

40. People you admire—Have I allowed certain people I admire to negatively influence my behavior, my thinking patterns, my sense of right and wrong, or my attitudes toward God, life, and others?

41. Romantic relationships—Have I allowed a romantic relationship in my life to negatively influence my behavior, my thinking patterns, my sense of right and wrong, or my attitudes toward God, life, and others?

42. Cultural norms—Have I allowed certain activities and behaviors that are acceptable to society (e.g., materialism, workaholism, premarital sexual activity) to negatively influence my behavior, my thinking patterns, my sense of right and wrong, or my attitudes toward God, life, and others?

Please keep in mind that this is not a comprehensive list of sins. Ask God's Spirit to guide you throughout this process and bring to mind issues in your life that may not be included in the preceding material. Also, it is important to know that this "house cleaning" process is not just a onetime effort. As Christians, we must continually attend to the ongoing process of keeping our inner life swept clean for our King. We highly recommend going through an internal examination process like the one above periodically throughout your life.

NOTES

1. Bishop Bardsley, quoted in Amy Carmichael, *Gold Cord* (London: Society for Promoting Christian Knowledge, 1947), 159–162.
2. Robert Browning, "Andrea del Sarto," quoted in Oswald Chambers, *My Utmost for His Highest* (New York: Dodd, Mead, and Company, 1935), 130.
3. Carmichael, *Gold Cord*, 8.
4. Andrew Murray, quoted in L. B. Cowman, *Streams in the Desert* (Grand Rapids, MI: Zondervan, 1996), 436.
5. Hebrews 11:33–34.
6. Luke 18:27.
7. Matthew 18:3.
8. A. W. Tozer, *The Best of A. W. Tozer* (Grand Rapids, MI: Baker Book House, 1978), 15.
9. Andrew Murray, quoted in V. Raymond Edman, *They Found the Secret* (Grand Rapids, MI: Zondervan, 1984), 88.
10. George Whitefield, quoted in Cowman, *Streams in the Desert*, 277.
11. 1 Peter 1:16.
12. Edman, *They Found the Secret*, 34.
13. Oswald Chambers, *The Complete Works of Oswald Chambers* (Grand Rapids, MI: Discovery House, 2000), 912.
14. Chambers, *Complete Works*, 875.
15. Galatians 3:24, KJV.
16. Matthew 5:48.
17. Galatians 2:19–20, paraphrase.
18. Charles Trumbull, quoted in Edman, *They Found the Secret*, 120.
19. Ibid., 5.
20. Ibid., 73–78.
21. Galatians 2:20.
22. Edman, *They Found the Secret*, 121–126.
23. Romans 8:37, KJV.
24. Edman, *They Found the Secret*, 123.
25. Ibid., 4.
26. Ibid., 34.

27. Colossians 1:26–27, KJV.
28. Goulburn, quoted in Cowman, *Streams in the Desert,* 221.
29. Ibid., 212.
30. John 15:4.
31. Brother Lawrence, *The Practice of the Presence of God* (New York: Oneworld Publications, 1999), 39–40.
32. Ibid., 73.
33. Matthew 6:33, paraphrase.
34. Lawrence, *The Practice of the Presence of God,* 47.
35. John 15:5.
36. Chambers, *Complete Works,* 406.
37. E. M. Bounds, *E. M. Bounds on Prayer* (New Kensington, PA: Whitaker House, 1997), 490–491.
38. Chambers, *Complete Works*, 107.
39. NASB.
40. Acts 17:11.
41. Matthew 6:24.
42. Romans 12:2.
43. T. Austin-Sparks, *The School of Christ* (Lindale, TX: World Challenge), 9.
44. Oswald Chambers, quoted in David McCasland, *Oswald Chambers: Abandoned to God* (Grand Rapids, MI: Discovery House, 1993), 20.
45. Philippians 3:19.
46. 1 Corinthians 9:27.
47. Psalm 57:8.
48. Amy Carmichael, *God's Missionary* (Fort Washington, PA: Christian Literature Crusade, 1939), 23.
49. Hudson Taylor, quoted in Edman, *They Found the Secret,* 6.
50. 1 Peter 5:7.
51. Philippians 4:7.
52. Theodore L. Cuyler, quoted in Cowman, *Streams in the Desert,* 334
53. John Wesley, quoted in Bounds, *E. M. Bounds on Prayer,* 510.
54. Josef Ton, *Suffering, Martyrdom, and Rewards in Heaven* (Wheaton, IL: The Romanian Missionary Society, 2000), 328–332.
55. Geoffery Hanks, *70 Great Christians* (Ross-shire, Scotland: Christian Focus Publications, 2000), 119–123.
56. Ibid., 299–303.

57. Hebrews 11:33–34.
58. Hebrews 11:35–38.
59. Amy Carmichael, *If* (Washington, PA: CLC Publications, 2001), 60.
60. R. A. Torrey, *The Best of R. A. Torrey* (Grand Rapids, MI: Baker Book House, 1991), 106–108.
61. St. Ignatius, quoted in Cowman, *Streams in the Desert,* 238.
62. 1 Corinthians 11:1, NKJV.
63. Charles Haddon Spurgeon, quoted in Cowman, *Streams in the Desert,* 283.
64. Acts 7:54–60.
65. Daniel 3:17–18.
66. Job 13:15, KJV.
67. Esther 4:16, NKJV.
68. WGBH Educational Foundation, "Sir Ernest Shackleton and the Endurance Expedition," *Shackleton's Antarctic Adventure,* http://main.wgbh.org/imax/shackleton/sirernest.html (accessed March 30, 2004).
69. Lawrence, *The Practice of the Presence of God,* 40.
70. G. D. Watson, *Tract #76* (Grand Rapids, MI: Faith, Prayer, & Tract League).

MORE TITLES BY ERIC AND LESLIE LUDY
FROM MULTNOMAH PUBLISHERS

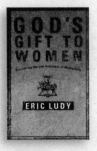

GOD'S GIFT TO WOMEN
In a culture that exalts the caveman-like qualities of masculinity, most women have stopped expecting anything more. More than ever, men need to know that they can rise above this sad mediocrity. With its riveting vision of Christ-centered manhood, *God's Gift to Women* shows young men how to become the heroic, selfless knight that every woman dreams about.

ISBN 1-59052-272-9

AUTHENTIC BEAUTY
In a world that seeks to destroy all that is princesslike and feminine within her, can today's young woman dare to long for more? For every young woman who has asked herself that question, this book explores the boundless opportunities God has for a young woman who is willing to let Him shape every aspect of her life.

ISBN 1-59052-268-0

WHEN DREAMS COME TRUE
In their bestseller *When God Writes Your Love Story*, Eric and Leslie Ludy offer fresh guidelines for being Christlike in relationships with the opposite sex. *When Dreams Come True* shares the Ludys' personal story, illustrating how they lived out the principles of the first book in their own romance and marriage.

ISBN 1-59052-303-2

WHEN GOD WRITES YOUR LOVE STORY
Lay the foundation now—whether you've met your future spouse or not—for a lifelong romance. Bestselling authors Eric and Leslie Ludy invite you to discover how beautiful your love story can be when the Author of romance scripts every detail.

ISBN 1-59052-352-0

DISCOVER A LOVE
WORTH WAITING FOR

ISBN 1-92912-527-5
$15.99

*Beautiful music by Eric and Leslie! This album powerfully
captures the journey of discovering a God-written love story.
To order your copy or download a free sample from this CD,
or for more information about
Eric and Leslie's ministry, please visit*

www.ericandleslie.com *or* www.authenticgirl.com.